Martinsburg, West Virginia and the

Great Railroad Strike of 1877

Todd Cimino-Johnson

Dedication page

This manuscript is dedicated to the men who decided to fight for what they believed in and to bring labor to a halt in Martinsburg in 1877. Their defiance is appreciated and not forgotten. It set the stage for other labor demonstrations up to and including our present time period.

Also, this book is dedicated to my grandmother, Helen. She would tell me about what life was like in Martinsburg when she was growing up before and during the Great Depression. Without her stories, I might not have loved history the way I do today.

Acknowledgements

I would like to acknowledge everyone who helped me find information for this book. The Martinsburg Public Library, Berkeley County Historical Society, Allison Seyler at the Baltimore and Ohio Railroad Museum in Baltimore, Nan Card at the Rutherford B. Hayes Presidential Library and my husband who did not see me for quite a long time, as well as family and friends. Additionally, I want to thank all those who taught me the value of education and to never give up on your dreams.

Authors Note

I was born and raised in Martinsburg, West Virginia. Until recently, I lived in Martinsburg. I grew up learning its history and understanding its people. It is a historical subject that I not only enjoy learning about but care genuinely about as well. The town of Martinsburg is over 200 years old. Its roots run deep for a small American town.

I tried to capture what life was like for those living in the 1870's. The records of the men who worked at Martinsburg for the B&O Railroad in 1877 are lost forever. A fire in the early 20th century destroyed all the known employee records of the 19th-century railroad employer. Their names may be forgotten, but they are not.

If you get a chance after reading this book, try to make a trip to the place where it occurred. One can only imagine what a sense of history was being made in July of 1877 at that spot. We can imagine how hot it was to be working in mid-summer and being paid less than the day before for the same amount of work.

Contents

Chapter 1-Introduction

The Great Railroad Strike of 1877 began in Martinsburg, West Virginia, on July 16, 1877. It was considered "great" because it spread across the United States at a fever pitch and touched just about every railroad line along the path. Each coast and all railroads in between were impacted, as well as other industries such as coal, textiles, and canals. Railroad lines as far away as San Francisco joined in the strike and let the voices of the people be heard. Some cities encountered destruction of either the town or rail yards. Martinsburg was not one of those places. Other than holding train cars and two men being shot, (with one eventually dying of his wounds,) it did not see the destruction other cities encountered.

With that said, Martinsburg is often overlooked regarding discussing the Great Railroad Strike of 1877. This book will conclude that because Martinsburg did not have the violence of other strike areas, it was ignored in the press when discussing the Great Strike of 1877.

1877 saw many issues and problems for the citizens of the United States. A severe and long-lasting depression had been impacting wages, rent, and prices for a few years. The Coinage Act of 1873 partly led to this depression. Robert Bruce stated, "Not only did a working man's daily wage fall at least 25 percent while the cost of food, consuming three-fifths of his pay, dropped only 5 percent; but also, longer and more frequent layoffs reduced his total yearly earnings even more."[1] This type of culminating crisis was just the type of powder keg being brought together for the events of 1877.

---

[1] Robert V. Bruce, *1877: Year of Violence* (Chicago: Quadrangle, 1970), Kindle Edition, Chapter 7.

Labor in the United States in the 19th Century had very few laws that protected workers. The government was mostly hands-off and pro-business. Four railroads were direct competitors to the Baltimore and Ohio in the Northeast. During the prior year, wages for workers were cut multiple times. As one railroad cut wages, the others followed suit. The problem with cutting wages at the expense of the worker was that the railroad companies were public and had actually made a profit according to the shareholder minutes and public newspapers of the time. The ongoing depression had cut into the profits of the railroad, and the companies wanted everyone, including the employees, to take their share of the cuts. Employees of the railroads knew that the companies had made a profit, yet lowered their wages several times. Newspapers though, before the issued pay cuts, had run stories on how well the railroads were doing. Pay for executive level positions were not affected and thus created a bitter taste in the mouths of the local railroad workers.

Workers grew tired of having to take pay cuts for the company's profit margins. Workers had not come together to strike on a mass scale up to this point in the nation's history. This was partly because not many labor unions were in existence at the time. Only four types of workers on the railroad had unions attached to them. They included the engineers, the firemen, the conductors, and the trainmen. Usually, unskilled laborers did not have a union. The issues were that they were more localized, connected by a common bond and not national in identity. Also, those different unions did not necessarily pull together and coordinate efforts at strikes or negotiation of wages. The unions' power was not consolidated and thus had little impact on the organization or for the workers themselves. Organization on a large scale was unusual because there was not an economy of scale to speak of at the time-strength in numbers. Labor unions were not that popular or widespread, and workers' rights were not protected by the government.

If the pay cuts could have saved the entire Baltimore and Ohio Railroad enterprise, the men would have understood. But the pay cuts were not helping to save the company, and the stockholders wanted a dividend. The pay cuts were due to greed on the part of the stockholders, especially one of its largest stockholders, President John W. Garrett. Mabel and Ann Gardiner stated, "In 1877 Mr. Garrett, president of the railroad since 1856, reported an unusual profit and congratulated the directors upon the immensity of its business during the previous year."[2] The board of directors had chosen to line their own pockets instead of making sure their employees were taken care of first. The mistake caused problems that the railroad did not anticipate, such as riots, strikes, and destruction of property.

---

[2] Gardiner, *Chronicles*, 177.

At the time of the wage cuts by the railroads, the competitors to the Baltimore and Ohio in the Northeast were the New York Central, the Erie, the Pennsylvania, and Hudson River. The Pennsylvania was the first to reduce wages by ten percent, followed quickly by the others. The Baltimore and Ohio were the last to reduce their wages among their major competitors. Edward Hungerford, the author of *The Story of the Baltimore and Ohio Railroad*, commented about the pay cuts that affected those on the B&O line by stating, "The Baltimore and Ohio was the last of the four to decide upon the drastic measure. John Garrett, President of the Baltimore and Ohio Railroad, was finally forced into it. On July 11, he issued a circular which stated that an immediate reduction had been made in the pay of all the officers and operators of the road whose wage was in excess of one dollar a day."[3] This reduction was a major decrease in the salaries of ordinary, blue-collar workers. This was not the first time these workers had seen pay cuts in the past year. The pay cut was as follows for firemen: first-rate firemen from $1.75 to $1.58 a day and second-rate firemen were reduced from $1.50 to $1.35 a day. In four years, 1873 until 1877, firemen on the Baltimore and Ohio Railroad had watched their wages decrease from "$55 a month to $30 in 1877; brakemen from $70 to $30, and conductors from $90 to $50."[4] It was greed and timing on the part of the executives of the railroad, to lower the wages of their employees while declaring dividends at the same time.

---

[3] Edward Hungerford. *The Story of the Baltimore and Ohio Railroad: 1827-1927.* (New York: Putnam, 1928) 133.

[4] Philip Foner, *The Great Labor Uprising of 1877*, (New York: Monad Press, 1979), 44.

The firemen of the B&O decided they had had enough pay cuts to their wages. They were the first of the unions to organize a strike. The Pennsylvania Railroad line of firemen had agreed to organize and hired professionals to help them achieve this goal. They decided that there had been enough pay cuts, and the men were not being treated fairly. The trainmen organized and made the decision to join the firemen and go on strike. Prices for rent and groceries had been increasing due to inflation, but the workers had only seen their pay decrease.

On July 14[th,] the decision had been made, and Martinsburg, West Virginia was chosen as the site of the first strike. The circular for pay cuts were to take effect on July 16th, 1877. This was the same day that the strikers decided they would walk off the job and abandon their shifts. Men from Baltimore to the east and Cumberland to the west arrived in the afternoon to join their brothers on this demonstration. A notice went out that said, "Notice had been given the crews of all trains, by the strikers, that after a certain hour no person should move an engine under penalty of death." [5] Up until this point, there had not been a significant strike in the nation, and especially one that would affect so many people. This line of the B&O not only serviced freight from all around the nation but along with it, mail, and people. With a shutdown of the line imminent, along with not knowing how long it might last, it would create a chain reaction of events around the country.

---

[5] Mabel Henshaw Gardiner and Ann Henshaw Gardiner. *Chronicles of Old Berkeley, a Narrative History of a Virginia County from Its Beginnings to 1926*. (Durham, NC: Seeman Press, 1938), 178.

The newly inaugurated President Rutherford B. Hayes had just been elected to office a few weeks before Inauguration Day on March 4, 1877. He was a Republican that had made a backroom offer to end Reconstruction in the South to become President. After his term began, he pulled the troops who had been stationed around the former Confederacy since the end of the Civil War, out of the South. This was a sign that President Hayes was not in favor of government intervention into what he believed were state matters. This did change when the governor of West Virginia asked for federal troops to quell the strike at Martinsburg in mid-July.

The governor of West Virginia was Henry Mason Mathews. He was a conservative, pro-business Democrat elected in 1876. Mathews was contacted when the strike broke out in Martinsburg by the mayor via telegraph, and he had been criticized by some for not asking for federal assistance sooner, which may have prevented a nationally led strike. At this time, the capital of West Virginia was in Wheeling, which was also along this same Baltimore and Ohio route. This was where Mathews sent and received telegrams from the mayor and others with updates about the strike, as well as contacting the president.

The strike would end only a few days after it started. What the uproar in Martinsburg caused was not just the unfairness of the labor pay, but much more underlying issues in American labor markets. Not only did the railroad lines strike, but also "Canal boatmen, miners and other workers turned out to redress their own grievances as well as to assist the railroad men."[6] The idea that these men were alone was preposterous. There were going to be many fights ahead between labor and capital.

---

[6] Philip S. Foner, *History of the Labor Movement in the United States, Vol 1: From Colonial Times to the Founding of the American Federation of Labor* (New York, International Publishers, 1947), 466.

There have been many books written on the subject of the Great Railroad Strike. Their focus has not been on Martinsburg in as much detail as other more populated cities. Philip S. Foner, in *The Great Labor Uprising of 1877,* states that the strike actually began at "Camden Junction, two miles from Baltimore, a critical point through which all trains leaving Baltimore for Washington or the west passed."[7] This event happened the day before the Martinsburg strike and only resulted in engineers abandoning their engines and leaving cars on the tracks. Foner does, however, give Martinsburg credit for being the first town to successfully coordinate a strike along the B&O rail line.

Richard Hofstadter, in *American Violence: A Documentary History,* mentions Martinsburg but focuses more on Pittsburgh. Since violence that happened in Pittsburgh did not occur in Martinsburg, he only mentions it starting in the town and moves on to discuss the death and destruction in Pennsylvania.

Michael Bellesiles, in *1877: America's Year of Living Violently* focuses on the fact that there was a union at Martinsburg, the Trainmen's, that helped to make Martinsburg the first railroad line to strike. Bellesiles states, "workers had begun gathering at the B&O dispatch office in Martinsburg, a key railroad junction, listening to reports of the quick crushing of the nascent strike in Camden Junction by Baltimore police."[8] He does not go into detail as to why Martinsburg was chosen, like the next author. Bellesiles' book focuses on Martinsburg being readied to strike and chosen for July 16th, the day of the wage cuts. He gives a good overview of the events that happened and that were quickly put down.

---

[7] Foner, *The Great Labor Uprising of 1877,* 43.

[8] Michael A. Bellesiles, *1877: America's Year of Living Violently* (New York: New Press, 2012). Kindle Edition, chapter 5.

Robert Bruce, in *1877: Year of Violence,* focuses on the Trainmen's Union and why Martinsburg was chosen to strike first. Bruce states, "It was a key railroad junction. It lay in West Virginia, which was not quite so well regulated a B&O satrapy as Maryland. The town's police force was small. And the citizens passionately supported the railroad workers."[9] The people of Martinsburg were against lavishness and people unlike them. It was a blue-collar town full of Scotch-Irish descendants, and thus the reaction was much different than in a larger city, such as Baltimore. With only 8,000 residents that were all connected in some way and highly favorable toward the worker, the outcome of such a strike turned out just as could be expected. Only one person died, and nothing was burned or looted.

Most of the writing concerning Martinsburg focuses on just the unionization. Whether it was weak or strong and how much influence it had on the strike seems to be the main focus. The reason history does not focus on Martinsburg as much as other cities have yet to be explored. Martinsburg began the strike, and if not for it, the Great Railroad Strike of 1877 may not have happened.

There are unexplored questions around the strike. For instance, why is Martinsburg not explored and discussed in more detail in most books on the subject? Who were the men that started the strike, and what were their motivations? How much of an impact did Martinsburg have on the rest of the nation? Why are the small towns overlooked when they create such a significant impact? Martinsburg did not have the wealth or population of cities that went on to strike and are discussed in greater detail. Still, Martinsburg plays the most pivotal role in that it did strike first, and that it did it in a manner that was both peaceful and impactful.

---

[9] Bruce, *1877, Year of Violence* (Chicago: Quadrangle, 1970), Kindle Edition, Chapter 7.

Martinsburg deserves more credit and more recognition for the role it played in the working man's life. Most history books written about the subject seem to forget that within the Shenandoah Valley lies one of the starting points for a year of violence. The genteel strike that started in Martinsburg and evolved into the Great Railroad Strike of 1877 is often overlooked by historians because it did not produce the death and damage upon the city, as strikes in Baltimore and Pittsburgh, which were wealthier and more affluent.

Chapter 2-The 1870's

The Great Railroad Strike of 1877 had implications not only in West Virginia but also around the country. The strike in Martinsburg set off a chain reaction from Baltimore to Pittsburgh, Albany, Saint Louis, Denver and all the way to San Francisco. This strike occurred along railroad lines and not only on Baltimore and Ohio lines. This strike occurred along all of them. The strike was the result of pent-up anger, fear, and loss around the lives of the workers. The strikers had suffered during the Civil War, the depression that hit in 1873, through worry and bewilderment during the election of 1876, and at home with decreased wages or even unemployment. An American can only be beaten down so much before he or she decides to fight back. That fight started in Martinsburg, West Virginia.

The chapter will address three areas related to the railroad strike and Martinsburg, West Virginia itself, on July 16, 1877. The first section will discuss research related to the power of the railroad. It seemed to have unlimited power when it came down to it. The second section examines the mood in Martinsburg in 1877 and the lives of the men who lived and worked there. The third section will focus on research studies about how much of an impact Martinsburg had on the rest of the nation concerning its small and uneventful strike. In the end, there were three days of workers on strike, with one striker dead and a local militiaman wounded. Martinsburg struck quickly and ended quickly. The impact though was felt throughout the nation.

The power of the railroad was something that most people would find to be unprecedented. Philip Foner wrote in *The Great Labor Uprising of 1877*, "By 1877, the railroad network consisted of over 79,000 miles. Overall, the industry represented an investment of almost $5 billion, nearly half of which ($2.26 billion) consisted of bonded debt. By way of comparison, the national debt that same year stood at $2.1 billion."[10] The railroad was the biggest business in the United States at this point in time. Railroads were carrying almost all of the troops, freight, people and mail around the country. Many Americans either worked for the railroads or benefited greatly from their operations. A railroad could pull out of a town and overnight the people were left with nothing. "Communities either flourished or disappeared at their whim. The railroad companies frequently owned the coal fields and the iron mines."[11] If people were going to live in a capitalistic society in 1877, they were now dependent upon the railroad for their livelihood. The size and strength of the railroad were felt not only in the economy but also in the government. "In some states, they were in complete control of the political machinery, and they were notorious for their rapport with high federal officials."[12] Not just in the federal government but in the state and local governments around the country, the railroads had made their dominance of the economy known. Since the government gave them the right to operate and to buy land or put in a track, railroads took this a step further and made sure to place those favorable to their side in office. Politicians were afraid to go against the railroad interests and to face their power. Doing so could be political suicide, as railroads had the money and will to have a seat replaced or a politician ousted that did not side with them.

---

[10] Foner, *The Great Labor Uprising*,16.

[11] Ibid., 17.

[12] Ibid.

Rutherford B. Hayes took the presidency on March 4, 1877. It is not coincidental that Hayes received this election at the hands of Thomas A. Scott, President of the Pennsylvania Railroad. So strong was the hand of the railroad in 1877, that a corporate president decided who became president of the United States. In return, Scott wanted the support of the Texas Pacific Railroad line being considered. When Hayes received word on March 2, 1877, that the special commission set up to figure out who was elected president had made their decision, Hayes was on Scott's own private rail car.[13] The railroad had entrenched itself throughout government to ensure that any new lines would receive approval from the highest office in the land.

The United States changed immensely after the Civil War. It went from a patchwork of small manufacturers, tradesmen and farmers to urban workers. Jeremey Brecher stated in his book, *Strike!*, "In 1860, only one-sixth of the American people lived in cities of 8,000 or more; by 1900 it was one-third. The number of wage-earners, meanwhile, grew from 1.5 million to 5.5 million. The United States became a full-fledged capitalist society with an economy driven by the pursuit of private profit in a virtually unregulated market."[14] The railroads were allowed to operate without any government intervention. The United States did not have the federal power and strength of a Theodore Roosevelt yet. They operated unchecked and were able to decrease wages, even if making a profit. The goal of the corporation was profit, and the bottom line was what mattered, no matter how many employees were let go or how much paychecks decreased. It was all in the name of capitalism.

---

[13] Ibid, 18-19.

[14] Jeremy Brecher, *Strike!* (Oakland, PM Press, 2014), 8.

Before the Civil War, there were not as many people working for corporations as there were in 1877. Thus, the idea of a strike was never really able to materialize. It took the economy that grew out of the Civil War to actually bring about the conditions for a nationwide strike to occur. Brecher stated that, "Railroads, factories and farms grew at breakneck speed in the years following the Civil War. What had been largely a local and regional economy became a truly national one."[15] There was now a collection of workers who shared a common enemy, the capitalistic organization. There was not yet a government that wanted to protect the worker since this idea was new in the United States. Before this time, most free people worked for themselves on farms or small business operations. The concept of large corporate entities had yet to happen. This all changed after 1865.

Without the railroads, there may not be the United States of America we know today. The railroad stretched the limits of American ingenuity and moved people and products quicker and farther than ever before. It opened vast tracks of land in the west that many people had not seen before. Gerald Eggert, in *Railroad Labor Disputes: The Beginning of the Federal Strike Policy*, argued that,

"The federal government's handling of railway strikes in the closing decades of the nineteenth century served to repress labor. In part this was due to prevailing notions of property rights and of laissez-faire government; in part it was the result of Congress' failure to deal effectivity with the emerging labor problem, leaving the executive and   courts to cope with strikes that had already become violent; and in part it reflected the interests and motivations of the men who made public policy."[16]

---

[15] Brecher, *Strike!*, 9.

[16] Gerald G. Eggert, *Railroad Labor Disputes: The Beginnings of Federal Strike Policy*. (Ann Arbor, University of Michigan Press, 1967), 22.

Eggert argues that railroads were a new economic catalyst that the federal government was ill-equipped to handle. At first, they wanted the matter to be handled in the private sector, without government interference. This was new territory for policy, and there were no prior laws. Eggert also argued that those in the government were not interested in handling railroad labor disputes because they benefited from them politically and financially. The government did not have a reason to become involved when this option could backfire and cost the politician re-election.

The railways in the 1870s had overtaken most industries to become the nation's most important economic engine. Even though President Hayes was deep in the pocket of the railroads, he was aware of their power. In August of 1877, he wrote in his journal, "the strikes have been put down by force; by now for the real remedy. Can't something [be] done by education of the strikers, by judicious control of the capitalists, by wise general policy to end or diminish the evil?"[17] Hayes understood that the strikers were not the issue. Greedy capitalists were also to blame for the situation that started in Martinsburg and spread around the country. When he sent federal troops first to Martinsburg, he was not taking a side, but only trying to prevent looting and destruction of private property. His main issue was that he was stuck in the middle of being seen as a champion of the laborers and having the money interest of the country turn against him, or siding with the railroads and having an angry population of voters destroy his political career. Neither was a viable option for President Hayes.

---

[17] Eggert, *Railroad Labor Disputes*, 55.

West Virginia is the only state that is set entirely in what is considered Appalachia. The Appalachian Regional Commission defines Appalachia as "a 205,000-square mile region that follows the spine of the Appalachian Mountains from southern New York to northern Mississippi. It includes all of West Virginia and parts of 12 other states."[18] A people should not be defined just by their location, though. For some, Appalachia is not a location, but an identity. J.D. Vance, in his autobiography, *Hillbilly Elegy,* states,

"I may be white but I do not identify with the WASP's of the Northeast. Instead, I identify with the millions of working-class white Americans of Scots-Irish descent who have not college degree. To these folks, poverty is the family tradition-their ancestors were day laborers in the Southern slave economy, sharecroppers after that, coal miners after that, and machinists and millworkers during more recent times. Americans call them hillbillies, rednecks, or white trash.[19]

---

18 "The Appalachian Region," The Appalachian Region - Appalachian Regional Commission, accessed April 09, 2017,
https://www.arc.gov/appalachian_region/theappalachianregion.asp.
    19 J.D. Vance, *Hillbilly Elegy: A Memoir of a Family and Culture in Crisis.* (New York, Harper Collings, 2016), 3.

A culture is made up of not only working conditions but music, art, religion, language, and social habits. The people who made up Martinsburg and the Berkeley County area had that unique connection. They were linked by their ties to a past that had not gone away with the Civil War or the railroad. From the beginnings of the American experiment until 1877, these families still inhabited the area of Martinsburg. They were the Mackeys, Faulkners, Seiberts, Smiths, Hess(e)s, Nolls, Stewarts, Henshaws, Evans, Boyds, Nadenbouschs, Vanmetres, Burkharts, Thompsons, Ganos, Thatchers and Millers.[20] These families had been in Berkeley County long before 1877 when the strike broke out. No doubt some of these families took part and identified as Appalachian.

Martinsburg began to thrive after the Civil War. Many new businesses were put into operation. During the vote for the final resting place of the state capital in 1877, a circular was put out to allow the fine establishments of Martinsburg as the possible site of the next capital. The circular stated, "assets catalogued for the benefit of state readers were a gas works to supply a population of 30,000; eleven churches, five public school buildings to take care of 2,500 pupils; two 'prosperous' seminaries; and five hotels, the newest on 'larger and in every respect more convenient than the Hale House in Charleston' with a total hotel capacity of 1,000 guests."[21] Martinsburg had grown in size and strength. To be considered one of three possible sites for the capital was an honor and privilege bestowed upon the city.

Berkeley County went from a population of 8,976 in 1860, to 10,312 in 1870 and 11,870 by 1880.[22] Even though the country was in a depression, people were still on the move looking for work, heading west or moving closer to the family.

---

[20] Evans, *Berkeley County*, 168-262

[21] Doherty, *Berkeley County*, 214.

Not only was Martinsburg becoming less agrarian, but it was also changing in shape to the times. With new jobs in manufacturing and on the railroad, the people changed, too. Allan Nevins details the change in *The Emergence of Modern American: 1865-1878*. He stated, "Clothing was altering to conform with the exigencies of a machine civilization. The ordinary man still had his best suit tailor-made of sooty broadcloth, but for everyday wear his suit was ready-made, and his shoes and congress gaiters came from the factory."[23] As industrial life changed, so, too, did the way in which Americans bought their clothes. Demand had increased for clothing, so the emergence of manufactured clothing took hold. At this time, meat began to appear on the tables of Americans like never before. With the invention of refrigerated railroad cars and the process for slaughtering increasing, the goods became cheaper to produce. "With large resulting gains in the cheapness and quality of the meats served on American tables. The local butcher, especially in the East, was thrust to the wall."[24] This was one of many processes to change after 1865 that changed the American household. In Martinsburg, the possibility existed that families were flush in new and cheaper, mass-produced goods such as beer, flour, pottery, farm equipment, or sewing machines. America had been growing up, and so, too, Martinsburg along with it.

[22] "West Virginia Population by Race," West Virginia Population by Race, 2015, accessed April 09, 2017, http://www.wvculture.org/history/teacherresources/censuspopulationrace.html.

[23] Allan Nevins, *The Emergence of Modern America*. (Chicago, Qudrangle Books, 1927), 44.

[24] Ibid, 37.

Since more people were being paid with money, they needed a safe place to deposit it. "In Massachusetts there were ninety-three savings banks in 1862, and one hundred and eighty in 1875."[25] The industrial changes brought about after the war also changed how Americans were paid and how they saved their money. Not only did banks rise in towns, but so did insurance companies. Allan Nevins, in *The Emergence of Modern America,* stated, "Insurance companies, many of them speculative ventures with insufficient capital, incompetent management and a shocking inattention to sound actuarial principles, rose on every hand."[26] It was the capitalistic way that when an economy started to expand, new services were needed. This was the America of 1877, even during a depression. New markets and new services were being offered in the country, as they were in Martinsburg.

Food in 1877 was anything but dull and ordinary. "The American diet altered but slowly. One of the principal changes was the more and more general introduction of oatmeal, called 'grits' or 'Irish Oatmeal' as a breakfast dish. It tended to lighten that repast, which still usually comprised not only fruit, coffee, and rolls but steak, chops or ham and eggs, and frequently in addition fried potatoes."[27] With the change in refrigeration and the railroad, more households now had access to meat at a lower price. The men of the strike could have been married with a family in 1877. Men and women married at young ages in 1877. Nevins states, "the ages of twenty-three for men and seventeen for girls were regarded as perfectly normal for contracting a union."[28] Families would have been started, and quite possibly, there were young children at home when the strike broke out.

---

[25] Ibid.,47.

[26] Ibid.

[27] Ibid., 210.

[28] Ibid., 215

Martinsburg sits on the dividing line between North and South. The sympathies during the Civil War were with the South in most corners of the county. "Sunday was generally observed with strictness throughout the Northern and Middle states. No theaters could open their doors; all liquor sales were forbidden though evasion was frequent; and businesses were tightly closed, even drug stores sometimes falling under the prohibition." [29] Religion, as well as a religious observance, was one of those traditions carried over. Martinsburg was one of those places that were slow to change, even as the state government did.

Since Martinsburg was not famous or fabulous, there are very few sketches written about the town and its surroundings in 1877. In 1888, Vernon Aler wrote the first-known history of Martinsburg and Berkeley County. In it, he describes it as such, "The streets are wide, and partly planted with Lombardy poplars, and have a very fine appearance. Eight taverns are kept in this place; one of them has the reputation of being one of the best in the United States and is well known by those who resort to the Warm Springs. Here is kept a coffee house, where, almost all the papers in the United States are read; 8 large stores, one printing office; there are also five public meeting houses of worship."[30] Martinsburg had a courthouse, jail, market house and city hall. All of them would have been repaired or rebuilt after the war due to the occupation during the Civil War.

---

[29] Ibid., 212

[30] F. Vernon Aler, *Aler's History of Martinsburg and Berkeley County, West Virginia.* (Hagerstown, The Mail Publishing Company, 1888), 375.

Even though times were tough, some people were getting along fine. Not all households were destitute or struggling. If some of the strikers were able, they might have had beautiful furniture, clothes and plenty of food. It is not inconceivable that some were supported by family and kept their jobs during the 1873-to-1877 period of the depression. If so, they would have had a more comfortable living than their coworkers. "In what we may call the typical American town or city home, the dwelling of a fairly well-to-do clerk or shopkeeper or businessman, there was better food, better furniture, better clothing, and more books and magazines."[31] This picture of a well-to-do clerk or shopkeeper represents some in Martinsburg in 1877.

Martinsburg's impact could only be seen as the match that lit the powder keg. Even though the reports coming out of Martinsburg were false concerning a riot, and that vandalism, violence, and murder were taking place, it helped to start the Great Railroad Strike of 1877. Before federal troops were called in to quell the strike in Martinsburg, it had spread. Philip Foner pointed out, "While the company and the Governor had been trying unsuccessfully to crush the strike at Martinsburg, it had spread to other points along the line in West Virginia; Keyser, Piedmont, Grafton, and Wheeling."[32] Workers within a day heard the news from Martinsburg and decided to strike while the time was right. There was no use to wait for another opportunity, and the time was now right for them to strike. On July 20th, a day after the strike was suppressed in Martinsburg, Foner stated that, "On the same day that the manifesto was posted, at Cumberland, Maryland, disgruntled miners, Chesapeake & Ohio canal men, railroad strikers, and unemployed workers uncoupled cars from a westbound freight train."[33] Martinsburg had started the momentum, and now, West Virginia, along the same rail line, was taking it further.

---

[31] Aler, *History of Martinsburg.*,203.

After Martinsburg, the workers were not finished. Their demands at Martinsburg had not been met, and they were still angry. Michael Bellesiles, in *1877: America's Year of Living Violently*, describes the thoughts of the men after Martinsburg. "Despite their defeat, workers met and resolved that they would rather "die by the bullet as starve to death by inches" and voted to continue their strike."[34] After two, ten-percent pay cuts, the workers were now deciding to continue to strike, rather than stay silent and starve. The strike continued down the line to other cities and towns.

---

[32] Foner, *Great Labor Uprising*,50.

[33] Ibid, 60.

[34] Michael Bellesiles, *1877: America's Year of Living Violently*. (New York, The New Press, 2010) Kindle Edition, Chapter 5.

The Great Strike of 1877 not only brought national attention to Martinsburg but to labor organizations as well, argues Norman Ware in *The Labor Movement in the United States: 1860-1895*. "The effect of the riots of 1877 was enormous. For the first time in America the head of labor revolution was raised. Until then, the labor movement had been ignored except by those in immediate contact with it."[35] Labor unions were not in vogue in 1877 and had a hard time getting traction. Organizations hired employees to infiltrate the unions and spy on anyone in attendance. The mines, iron works, and railroads where unions attempted would either fire the employees or harass them into submission to remove themselves from the union. Philip Foner sums up the feeling of workers in *History of the Labor Movement*, by saying, "Not even the docile and fraternal organizations of railroad workmen, the Brotherhood of Railway Conductors and the Brotherhood of Locomotive Firemen and Enginemen, were tolerated by the companies. Union men were blacklisted, grievance committees were refused hearings, and the Pinkerton spies were so active that workers were afraid to talk to one another."[36] Labor had been under attack, but that all seemed to change after Martinsburg. After Martinsburg, the labor idea and consciousness awoke. They did not take off immediately, but the ordinary worker could now see how vital a labor union could benefit them. The labor union could supply the much-needed voice for the everyday worker.

---

[35] Norman Ware, *The Labor Movement in the United States: 1860-1895*. (New York, Random House, 1929), 48.

[36] Foner, *History of the Labor Movement*, 464.

As news of the strike spread, other people began to stand up. Even though Martinsburg did not convince the Baltimore and Ohio to reverse the ten-percent wage cut, it was successful in that it did something rather than nothing. The almost four days of non-movement of trains and little intervention helped to propel others to join in. As Page Smith said, in *The Rise of Industrial America: A People's History of the Post-Reconstruction Era,* "Word of strikes and wild demonstrations came from Philadelphia, Columbus, Ohio, Chicago, Cincinnati, and St. Louis. The initial success of the strikers in stopping the movement of freight and the apparent incapacity of the railroads, the militia, and even the Federal troops to get the trains moving emboldened the strikers."[37] The impact that Martinsburg had on these workers was felt not just locally, but now, nationally. The news spread far and wide that Martinsburg had made a stand that could be replicated elsewhere. It was done without the destruction of private property or public property. It was a show of force that could be imitated in city after city.

The strike that began in Martinsburg and went nationwide left a profound effect on both people and the nation. Page Smith goes on to say," When John Swinton looked back from the perspective of the 1890's, it seemed to him that the Great Strikes had been a landmark."[38] No one person could have predicted that a small band of railroad men in a small city in West Virginia would create a cascade effect that would touch every major city in the United States and lots of smaller ones. This is the era before the telephone, and the telegraph was not stationed in every household. News and word of the strike were so thrilling that it found its way around the nation.

---

[37] Page Smith, *The Rise of Industrial America: A People's History of the Post-Reconstruction Era.* (New York, Penguin Books, 1984), 170.

[38] Smith, *Industrial America,* 189.

The end result of the strike that started in Martinsburg seemed to be lost. Page Smith tells the reader, "In the aftermath of the Great Strikes the Baltimore & Ohio instituted a program to assist the families of the victims of disabling accidents. The Relief Association, adapted from British models, was a form of insurance into which workers paid a fee that provided for them and their families in case of injury, illness, or death."[39] What began as a small strike in Martinsburg and went nationwide, changed the Baltimore and Ohio policies. Not only did they provide insurance, but a retirement system was set up to provide fifty-percent retirement pay. The benefits that companies gave to their employees grew in time, especially after the post-World War Two era. For a brief time, Martinsburg impacted not only the nation but the operations of the railroads.

The railroads, as shown, were very powerful and unchecked by the federal government. They were able to move almost all the freight and goods across the country, move people, mail, and have favorable politicians elected or not. Since they went from little power to much power in a matter of years, the government had failed to rein in this influence. It was too late in July of 1877 to take the side of the workers on the railroads because of this unbridled power grab. It would take years before the railroads began to lose their grip on the government and for the government to pass laws favorable to the workers.

---

[39] Ibid., 191.

Martinsburg was small but essential to the railroad in 1877. It was a hub for all traffic heading west, and it was necessary to pass through. When Martinsburg stopped all traffic in July of 1877, it made a statement that the Baltimore and Ohio could not ignore. There was not another way around it, and only by passing through Martinsburg could freight be worth anything. The streets of Martinsburg were unpaved in 1877 when the strike broke out. The city was not quite 8,000 people, but they were a rabble group of German and Scotch-Irish ancestry that was not afraid to stand up for their rights. Their power lay in the fact that they were sticking together and not backing down from a fight.

The impact of Martinsburg cannot be diminished. Looking at the domino effect that Martinsburg started only shows how great the work stoppage was in Martinsburg. Neither train nor freight was moved, but the sympathizers around the nation were indeed moved to action. The powerful statement that was made in Martinsburg helped other workers of not only railroads but of the canals, mines, and iron, to find their voices and rise up. Martinsburg set the stage for what was not only a strike but the Great Strike of 1877. Every industry that had employees was now engaged from all regions of the United States. The scene across the nation was that of unity as worker after worker rose up and joined his fellow man in resisting greed and capital, and demanding fairness and a livelihood.

Chapter 3-Background

To discuss the Great Railroad Strike of 1877, more background into where it took place and who was involved is explored. Martinsburg is the county seat of Berkeley County in the eastern part of West Virginia. It is located at what is considered the beginning of the Shenandoah Valley. The Blue Ridge Mountains set the scene against the backdrop of this blue-collar town. Martinsburg was founded by Adam Stephen in 1778. It is very much set out like a Scottish town in the manner its founder intended.

Berkeley County, and especially Martinsburg, was made up of a mix of different European backgrounds. The great-grandchildren and great-great-grandchildren of the original European inhabitants would eventually work on the railroad and become a part of the Great Strike of 1877. German, Irish, Scotch-Irish, and English made up the majority of the population when it was initially settled, with the two largest being German and Scotch-Irish. James Leyburn, in *The Scotch-Irish: A Social History*, describes the immigrants from Northern Ireland, "as quick-tempered, impetuous, inclined to work by fits and starts, reckless, too much given to drinking. No contemporary observer praised them as model farmers." [40] They were not the most dependable or well-liked individuals and loved to fight. The Germans, on the other hand, were the opposite. They were peaceful, pious and hardworking, hardly ever resorting to drinking or fighting. "It was usual to expect Germans to be orderly, industrious, carefully frugal."[41] Even though they were more industrious, their heirs would bond with the Scotch-Irish only a few generations later and help to start a labor strike in the county in which they tried to live and work separately.

---

[40] James G. Leyburn, *The Scotch-Irish: A Social History*. (The University of North Carolina Press, 1962) 191.

On February 28, 1827, the Maryland Legislature laid the tracks for what became a center of industry for decades, the Baltimore and Ohio Railway.[42] The original intention was to connect Baltimore by train through the Shenandoah Valley to the Kanawha River and finally, to the Ohio Valley. Virginia agreed to this line only if it was north of the Kanawha Valley, thus cutting what would be Southern West Virginia out of the line. It was then decided to bring the line more north, through Maryland and into Virginia through Berkeley and Jefferson County, in present-day West Virginia. Because of disagreements with the Chesapeake and Ohio Canal, which paralleled this line and was in competition with the railway, the project was stopped at Point of Rocks, Maryland for three years with legal battles and right of way issues. [43] With a change in political party affiliation in 1838, the newly elected Democrats of Virginia did not let the project proceed any further.[44] In 1840, the tide switched again, and the train was carried forward. The Martinsburg Gazette predicted that the train would arrive on Thursday, July 18, 1839, to excited residents and businesses in Martinsburg, but it was another few years before it actually arrived. The first train to arrive in Martinsburg blowing smoke and its horn was not until 1842.[45]

---

[41] Ibid.

[42] William Doherty, *Berkeley County, U.S.A: A Bicentennial of a Virginia and West Virginia County, 1772-1972* (McClain Printing Company, 1976) 114.

[43] Ibid.
[44] Ibid.

[45] Ibid., 115.

Martinsburg and the country were transformed by the railway's new means of transportation. Industry in Martinsburg grew, and new jobs were created when engine houses and machine shops were needed to fix train cars.[46] Along with the newly generated industry, a state- of-the-art Depot House Hotel was built which accommodated many visitors who traveled along the tracks. Additionally, other hotels were built near the station but did not survive the Civil War. Martinsburg and Berkeley County reaped the reward of having the Baltimore and Ohio major railway line cut through the town and link the northern, southern, eastern and western portions of the country.

When war broke out in 1861, the Baltimore and Ohio Railway junction in Martinsburg became a prized jewel for both the North and South. As a result, conflict, and war ensued in and around Martinsburg. Martinsburg was situated on the Potomac River, which is the dividing line between the North and the South. By April of 1861, Confederate armies under the direction of Thomas J. "Stonewall" Jackson took control of the railroad line from Point of Rocks, Maryland all the way through Morgan County, Virginia, (to become West Virginia in 1863,) therefore seizing the critical junction of Martinsburg while controlling the movement of supplies, materials and goods to all points North, South, East and West.[47] By doing so, Jackson cut off coal routes from Cumberland, Maryland that supplied both Baltimore and Washington D.C., making it difficult for the Union to garner much-needed supplies to win the war.[48]

[46] Mabel and Ann Gardiner, *Chronicles of Old Berkeley: A Narrative History of a Virginia County from Its Beginnings to 1926* (Seeman Press, 1938) 166-167.

[47] Doherty, *Berkeley County*, 141.

[48] Ibid.

By mid-1861, General Jackson clearly understood that the Martinsburg junction and the Baltimore and Ohio Railroad line was vital to the Union. He knew that this line must be destroyed in case the Union won back the area. In June of 1861, General Jackson destroyed a colonnade bridge that spanned the town of Martinsburg.[49] The bridge was donated by the Baltimore and Ohio Railroad when the line came through Martinsburg as a thank you to the city for their generosity. In addition to the destruction of a critical bridge, he destroyed 35 locomotives by running them off the same bridge that had been destroyed.[50] Leaving only a few locomotives for the South, he hauled them via 30-40 horses to the Winchester Toll Pike through Winchester, Virginia and finally put them back on the tracks in Strasburg, Virginia, therefore claiming the northern locomotives for the South. Once the war was over, it was not until 1867 when the rail lines in Berkeley County, Virginia, (which became West Virginia in 1863,) were completely repaired, and a new smaller bridge was built that once again joined commerce from the North, South, East, and West.

The Baltimore and Ohio Railroad line and the junction in Martinsburg became a significant reason why Jefferson, Berkeley, and Morgan counties were annexed by the state of West Virginia, a Union State, and not Virginia, a Confederate state. When West Virginia was approved by the voters in 1862, neither Berkeley nor Jefferson were a part of the map. On the second vote that year, both of the counties were added and signed into law by Abraham Lincoln on December 31, 1862. It was not until 1871 in the case of *Virginia v. West Virginia* that the Supreme Court re-drew the map and declared that Jefferson, Berkeley and Morgan counties would officially be recognized as the Eastern Panhandle of West Virginia and not a part of Virginia.

---

[49] Ibid.
[50] Ibid.

During Reconstruction, Berkeley County and the Baltimore and Ohio Railroad line rebuilt the railroads that Jackson had destroyed. In addition to rebuilding, new railroad companies contributed to the expansion of Martinsburg while introducing new routes for passengers and commerce. Martinsburg was revitalized by the end of the Reconstruction, and the railroad industry was booming once more, bringing much-needed jobs and industry to the area. Martinsburg was revived beyond what it was before the war by the demands of the people. "Martinsburg slowly changed from a small agricultural and trading center to a thriving town whose importance was largely due to its location, and to the genius and public spiritedness of its citizens, who labored diligently to increase the methods of transportation."[51]

---

[51] Gardiner, *Old Berkeley*, 177.

Berkeley County and Martinsburg served as the thoroughfare between the Union and Confederate forces in the Civil War. Martinsburg changed hands thirty-seven times during the war and saw a lot of fighting each time it changed hands. Due to its location, it served not only as a major railroad depot but also as a hospital. When the Confederates lost the Battle of Antietam, many soldiers were moved on to Martinsburg since it was safely in rebel hands at the time. When soldiers from Gettysburg retreated to the South, the first major city they encountered in warm hands was Martinsburg. William Doherty said, "destruction exacted its toll during four long years of occupation. The Baltimore and Ohio Railroad was destroyed and rebuilt many times; churches and public buildings were converted into hospitals, barracks, or stables, and on occasion, these went up in flames due to the carelessness of the occupants. Business and government services were suspended, particularly during the early days of the war."[52] Even some of the courthouse records were destroyed by either side of the skirmishes. After the war, the town of Martinsburg went through a period of having to clean up and bring the town back to good order and open for business. This would take several years and lots of money to achieve.

---

[52] Doherty, *Berkeley County*, 161.

In early 1873, the United States experienced one of the most severe and long-lasting depressions it had ever witnessed to that point in time. Eric Foner states, "the Panic of 1873 ushered in what until the 1930's was known as the Great Depression, a downturn that lasted, with an intermittent period of recovery, nearly to the end of the century." [53] With the collapse of the banking system, so, too, went the bond market of the railroads. It was calamitous for the economy and the working man who endured year after year of either not having a job or having a wage cut for doing the exact job. Foner goes on to say, "By 1876 over half the nation's railroads had defaulted on their bonds and were in the hands of receivers." [54] The railroads were hit hard during the depression. The quick expansion was paid for by speculators who set up a system that was bound to collapse. To survive, expenses had to be cut, jobs lost, prices increased, and the blue-collar and unskilled workers suffered tremendously. This caused widespread demonstrations around the country and demands for work and or public works.

---

[53] Eric Foner, *Reconstruction: America's Unfinished Revolution, 1863-1877* (NY, NY: Harper Perennial, 2014), Kindle, chapter 11.

[54] Foner, *Reconstruction*, Kindle, Chapter 11.

Labor and capital were colliding due to longer work hours, less pay and lack of jobs. Mines in the Midwest saw many violent days as workers fought back against wage cuts. Their demonstrations did little to aid their efforts. In 1875, some textile workers in New England were on strike after they saw two cuts of ten percent each in their wages. Capital won out, and the workers returned to work with less than what they started with. In that same year, there was a strike known as the "long strike of 1875." Philip Foner says, "The defeat of the textile workers came shortly after an equally crushing defeat suffered by the miners."[55] Miners became agitated when their wages were cut over and over again by the Philadelphia and Reading Coal and Iron Company. The owner, Franklin B. Gowen, in a bid to have a reason to abolish the union attached to the company, decided to keep reducing wages until the workers would go on strike. When they did, he used this as an excuse to remove the union from the company and replaced all the workers. Anthracite coal was essential to the households around the country especially during the winter, and he knew it would not do well for business to allow the talk of a strike to threaten profits. These are a few of the most significant strikes to happen prior to 1877 and during the depression of the 1870s. Their impact was felt for a long time and did not escape the mind of other workers who would strike later in the decade. The election of 1876 did little to ease the tension of the average American.

---

[55] Philip Foner, *History of the Labor Movement in the United States, vol. 1* (New York: International Publishers, 1998), 455.

In 1876, the people of the United States observed one hundred years of freedom as the centennial of the Declaration of Independence had arrived. In Philadelphia, America celebrated the Centennial Exposition to mark the anniversary, and it became known as the first World's Fair. It included inventions such as typewriters, sewing machines, agricultural equipment, and a monorail. Many nations participated and sent their displays of inventions and culture to the United States. Alexander Graham Bell's telephone invention was on display for people to see how communication would one day work. The arm and torch of the not-yet-completed Statue of Liberty were on display for all to see. New foods on display included bananas, root beer, popcorn, and Heinz Ketchup. The United States should have been more celebratory, but it was not, due to the ongoing depression. "After weathering the cataclysm of the Civil War, Americans were confident that the country was about to fulfill its destiny as a nation that extended without interruption from the Atlantic to the Pacific. Little did they suspect that in just three days they would learn that the command of General George Custer, the greatest Indian fighter of them all, had been annihilated by the Lakota and Cheyenne."[56] The news came like a pile of bricks for the Americans celebrating the birth of the nation across the country. The fighting took place from June 25th to June 26th, but news of the calamity did not reach back east until July 4th. Custer and over 250 men were killed in the battle. It was a blow to the already downtrodden American's psyche.

---

[56] Nathaniel Philbrick, *The Last Stand: Custer, Sitting Bull and the Battle of Little Bighorn.* (New York, Penguin Group, 2010),287

In 1876, the Republican Party selected Ohio Governor, Rutherford B. Hayes, as their nominee for President of the United States. The Democrats chose New York Governor, Samuel J. Tilden, as their nominee. The election would end up fiercely contested almost until the inaugural. Once the ballots were counted nationwide, Tilden ended up with a popular vote total over Hayes. The issue came down to electoral votes as the Constitution calls for the election of a President. Florida, South Carolina, and Louisiana were all too close to call on who won the electors of those states. There were accusations of stuffed ballot boxes and other forms of cheating to increase vote totals for both candidates. Since the House of Representatives was solidly Democratic, and the Senate Republican, neither one could agree on how to proceed with this constitutional crisis. Eventually, in January, a 15-member Electoral Commission was created to settle the election. Made up of both Democrats and Republicans, the commission settled the matter by awarding the electoral votes to Hayes. It is thought that a backroom deal was cut and that Hayes agreed to remove the remaining federal troops from the South in exchange for the presidency. This disputed election lasted until March 2, 1877, only two days before a new president was to be sworn into office. On March 4th, 1877, Rutherford B. Hayes became the nineteenth President of the United States and officially ended Reconstruction a few months later.

In 1877, it was decided by the legislature to allow the people of West Virginia to choose where the final resting place of the capital should be located. Their choices were Clarksburg, Charleston or Martinsburg. On August 8, 1877, less than a month after the Martinsburg railroad strike, the voters went to the polls. West Virginia had moved its capital from Wheeling to Charleston and back to Wheeling in a matter of a decade. It was decided by the governor and the State House that the people should get the final say in their state capital. Martinsburg came in dead last. "Charleston received 41,243 votes; Clarksburg, 29,942; and Martinsburg badly trailed with 8,046." [57] Since Martinsburg was so far east from the other locations, it would not have made sense to have it as the capital. The counties that voted in favor of Martinsburg were Berkeley, Jefferson, and Morgan, with the last two bordering it, and with Martinsburg located within the boundary of Berkeley. Even though Martinsburg was chosen as a possible site for the capital and one that would have served the state well, the mood of the city must have been that of defeat as the railway workers lost their right to strike in July, and Martinsburg lost out to be the state capital in August. The overall anxiety felt by not just Americans but West Virginians played into the anxieties of workers and those unemployed. Political discord, a depression, and a memory of a civil war would have been enough to make any one person depressed.

---

[57] Doherty, *Berkeley County*, 217.

The Governor of West Virginia at the time of the strike was Henry Mason Mathews. He attended the University of Virginia and later became a major in the Confederate army, serving the state of Virginia during the Civil War. He was elected in 1865 to serve in the State Senate. The state had set up a voter test oath to not allow former Confederate soldiers to serve in the West Virginia government. Since the state had voters test oaths, he was not allowed to take the seat. Mathews became what was considered the first of the Bourbon Governors of West Virginia. The term Bourbon meant that he was a Democrat with strong ties to the Confederacy and the southern way of life. This also meant he was conservative and promoted trade and industry within the state.

Governor Mathews was very favorable to business and trade. His term was marked by using the resources of the state to entice business to locate within the border. Otis Rice discussed this in *West Virginia: The State and its People*, "Mathews also knew that industries liked to know what kind of resources a state maintained. He therefore encouraged the legislature to provide money for a state geological survey. The purpose of the geological survey was to provide accurate information about the minerals of West Virginia, such as coal, oil, gas, salt and iron ore."[58] Mathews was thinking about the economy and looking for ways to bring business into the state.

---

[58] Otis K. Rice, *West Virginia: The State and Its People*. (McClain Printing Company, Parsons, 1972),214.

Mathews' strong tie is felt during the strike as he was in contact with the president of the Baltimore and Ohio Railroad instead of siding with the strikers. Mathews also was an advocate of bringing in cheaper labor from Europe. He advocated for laborers from both Germany and Switzerland during his term to work in the coal mines, salt mines, gas wells, and other industries throughout West Virginia. Mathews wanted West Virginia to have a favorable business climate with the best workers that could be found and an economy that thrived even if the people were trampled over.

The 19th President of the United States played a pivotal role in breaking the strike in Martinsburg. Rutherford B. Hayes' action of sending federal troops was unprecedented. The country was essentially one hundred years old, and federal troops had been called out only once during the term of Andrew Jackson for a non-war issue. Hayes grew up in Ohio, the son of a man who died before he was born and a strong-willed mother, surrounded by an extended family. As a boy, "Rud," as he was called at that time, was very sickly. A person who influenced Rutherford was his uncle, Sardis Birchard, who was a firm believer in education. Being a banker and businessman as well as a lifelong bachelor, he managed to guide young "Rud" toward education and oversaw some of his upbringings. Sardis even went as far as financing part of his education and corresponding with schoolmasters. In one letter, Isaac Webb, schoolmaster of Middletown, Connecticut where Hayes studied, wrote this letter to Sardis, "Rutherford has applied himself industriously to his studies and has maintained a constant and correct deportment. I think he will avail himself of the advantage of an education and fully meet the just anticipation of friends. He is well informed, has good sense, and is respected and esteemed by his companions."[59] These traits would serve Hayes later in life when he became President of the United States. Hayes continued his climb in life from studious youth to lawyer, a fighter in the Civil War reaching the rank of Major General, and then he became a politician. During his time at Kenyon College, he started a diary and never stopped writing about his life until the day he died.

---

[59] Hans L. Trefousse, *Rutherford B. Hayes: The American President Series: The 19th President, 1877-1881*. (Times Books, New York, 2002), Kindle Edition, Chapter 1.

Hayes' time in the military gave him a lot of exposure to West Virginia, Virginia, and Ohio. If any one man knew the railroad, it was Hayes. He fought at Winchester, South Mountain, and passed through Martinsburg on more than one occasion going to and from battle. His study of the law at Harvard gave him an acumen about not only the law but the Constitution. As President, he made decisions that impacted everyday Americans. One of those was the decision to send federal troops to stop a railroad strike. Hayes understood what his order meant since he knew and understood the law, even fighting through a rebellion of not just a hundred men, but fourteen states.

To say John W. Garrett was an unknown personality in business would be an understatement. As President of the Baltimore and Ohio Railroad Company, he left his mark on the company after twenty-six years. Edward Hungerford writes in *The Story of the Baltimore and Ohio Railroad 1827-1927*, that, "the entire history of the railroad could be divided into three main epochs: before-Garrett, Garrett, and after-Garrett."[60] Not unlike other railroads that were considered the persona of the President, Garrett was no different. He ruled the Baltimore and Ohio with an iron first but could also be well-liked and charming. Hungerford goes on to describe his personality, "He possessed all the great qualities of leadership. He had, when he needed it, real charm. He could, upon occasion, be as tactful and as diplomatic, as he was upon other occasions, brusque and commanding. Seemingly, he could bend as easily as he could remain firm; and he was the personification of firmness itself." [61] Garrett's feeling toward the men who would stop his company was not seen as assets but liabilities. Hungerford, in the book stated above, mentions how Garrett was a leader, and along with that he could make cold hard business decisions that meant not putting the people first, but the bottom line.

---

[60] Edward Hungerford, *The Story of the Baltimore and Ohio Railroad: 1827-1927, vol. 1*

Captain Charles J. Faulkner was in charge of the local militia at the time of the railroad strike in 1877, but he did not start there. He was called upon and trusted not just because of his command but also because of his political past and ties to the State Democrats. At age eight, Charles was left an orphan with two Martinsburg citizens. They saw that he went to school, and he eventually graduated from Georgetown University. He began the study of law afterward in Winchester, Virginia, and was ultimately admitted to the Berkeley County Bar Association. Willis F. Evans had this to say about Faulkner, "[his]lot seemed always to be cast in rough places but these vicissitudes of fate seemed to be an asset to his career rather than a liability."[62] Faulkner went on to serve in prominent roles, even when choosing the wrong side of history.

(New York: Putnam, 1928),322.

[61] Hungerford, *Baltimore and Ohio*, 330.

[62] Willis F. Evans, *History of Berkeley County West Virginia*. (Bowie, Heritage Books, 2001), 171.

Charles Faulkner began his political career in 1832 in the Virginia House of Delegates, in 1841 in the Virginia Senate, and in 1848 in the Virginia House of Delegates again. In 1850, the state of Virginia held a reform Constitutional Convention and Faulkner was appointed a member. Western Virginia had many grievances against the East, and this was a time for western Virginia to try to air them. Faulkner was able to do that and try to help to even the playing field regarding taxes and counting slaves. Although western Virginia did not get all they wanted, it was a start and Faulkner was able to help. In 1851, Faulkner was elected to the United States Congress from Virginia. For his service to the Democratic Party and to President Buchanan's election in 1856, Faulkner was appointed Minster to France by the president in 1859. After President Lincoln was elected in 1860, Faulkner came home from France and was relieved of his duty as minister. He was immediately arrested in Washington D.C. for being a citizen of the rebel state of Virginia. He eventually was freed after an exchange was issued with the Confederates for another prisoner.

Stonewall Jackson made Faulkner his Chief of Staff and Lieutenant Colonel upon his return home to Martinsburg. Faulkner held this rank until the end of the war when he returned once more to Martinsburg. During the Supreme Court case of *Virginia v. West Virginia*, Charles Faulkner defended West Virginia's claim to both Berkeley and Jefferson County in present-day West Virginia. He won this case for West Virginia. These two counties were disputed by both Virginia and West Virginia because of the location of the Baltimore and Ohio Railroad. When West Virginia was formed in 1861 through 1863, these two counties were included. Faulkner's political life did not end with his service before the war in the Confederate Army. In 1872, he was appointed to the West Virginia Constitutional Convention when the Democrats took control of the government. In 1874, he was elected to serve West Virginia in the United States House of Representatives. With his run in 1876 to be a Senator from West Virginia, he was defeated and never served in a political capacity again. [63] Faulkner had a colorful career in politics and in law. He served both Virginia and West Virginia, presidents and governors, and was considered a patriot even though he sided with the Confederacy during the War of the States.

---

[63] Evans, *Berkeley County*, 171-174.

Martinsburg and the people who made up the city and county had come through a lot to survive. It was no easy task to live day to day in the 19th century, let alone the toil of war, a depression, a state in crisis and a constant struggle of living. The events that made up the period of 1860 to 1877 really shaped how the railroad strike evolved and why it evolved. Not one single event can be blamed for the strike, but like most events, it was the buildup to what would occur. The people, the place, and the time set the stage for the beginning of what would become the labor movement in the United States. In small-town America and not in industrial city America, the beginning of the unionization and labor struggles came head to head. The union growth continued until it was broken in 1922 in southern West Virginia, but for a time it had emerged and made its presence known.

Chapter 4- Strike at Martinsburg!

The year 1877 is not a year that most Americans know historically unless they are historians and, would never remember as significant concerning the history of the United States. It is not the start of the nation nor the end of the Civil War. It is the end of Reconstruction, not as well-known an event. Yet, it has much significance to the next one hundred years in the history of the United States. The real clash between labor and capital started in the year 1877 and set the stage for the unions, capital and strike policy in the country. Just like the year 1877 is lost, so, too, is Martinsburg, West Virginia the scene of where the collision of capital, labor, and the government met to decide the fate of what was to come.

Martinsburg has been the source of many developments. The most notable has been the Great Strike of 1877. This strike produced a domino effect upon the nation that created chaos, mayhem, and destruction in some cities and bewilderment in others. The wage cuts that railroads and other industries had inflicted upon their employees were too much for the citizens to take during the depression. This had been after the railroad decided to "obtain more work for less pay had been introduced. Extra cars, reduced crews, and no overtime pay for Sunday work"[64] had been experimented with at the railroad yards. Not to mention the railroads were charging much-inflated prices for workers to stay at railroad hotels and the doubling of train cars being put on an engine. To add insult to injury, the workers were not paid their salaries for June 1877 until mid-July. The workers at Martinsburg decided that they had enough and halted all train traffic and demanded that until the ten-percent pay cuts that took effect that day were restored, no trains would move out of the roundhouse or through the city.

---

[64] William Thomas Doherty, *Berkeley County, U.S.A.: A Bicentennial History of a*

The events leading up to this moment were a domino of moments. The depression had the most bearing on events that transpired. The railroads saw an opportunity to reduce wages and thus increase profits. Not one, but all four major railroads in the East, decided this was an excellent opportunity. In May, the Pennsylvania Railroad reduced wages by ten percent followed by The Erie and New York Central. The Baltimore and Ohio waited until the others had cut their wages to follow suit. The railroads had waited to see if the economy would turn around, so they did not have to take the measure of reducing the employees' pay.[65]

The other issue of the day was the attitude toward the railroads. In America, they were not very well liked or written about in the newspaper with flattery or praise. "Many people in America bitterly hated the railroads. Rate discriminations against individuals, firms and whole communities; stock manipulation, bribery, corruption, and the wholesale robbery of the public domain had so infuriated the people that they welcomed the chance to aid the strikers."[66] Just as the people and newspapers in Martinsburg took sides with the workers, the rest of the nation would do the same. All of the grievances against the railroads were not making them any friends other than in the Executive Mansion in Washington, D.C.

Virginia and West Virginia County, 1772-1972. (Parsons, McClain Printing, 1972), 223.

[65] Edward Hungerford, *The Story of the Baltimore and Ohio Railroad: 1827 to 1927.* (New York, Putnam, 1928), 133.

[66] Philip S. Foner, *History of the Labor Movement in the United States Vol. 1.* (New York, International Publishers, 1947), 465.

On the morning of Monday, July 16[th,] the ten-percent pay wage cut went into effect. It was considered a new schedule of wages by the railroad company, but to the workers, it was a greedy death knell. The workers in Martinsburg showed up and performed their duties just as the executives in Baltimore did. With the ongoing depression, it was expected that the wage cuts would be absorbed by the men in exchange for still having a job. The executives who made the decision to increase profits over the livelihood of men were wrong to assume such a stance.

The first sign of deteriorating conditions occurred at Camden Junction, just outside of Baltimore. Workers began to abandon the train cars and refused to move them. The local police were called in and arrested the men. Their plan was most likely not to coordinate a strike but just to abandon the cars in protest of their wage cuts. They did not anticipate violence but only protest. Willis Evans said, "On July 16th, early in the morning, a number of train hands left Baltimore and came to Martinsburg, while those idle from the west began to pour into town."[67] Since the Baltimore work stoppage did not succeed, the men decided to move up the line which was six hours by train, putting them there in the evening that same day.

The events at Martinsburg were more coordinated and not just a happenstance. "The Trainmen's Union included practically all the railroad workers in Martinsburg."[68] The Trainmen's Union had only been started on June 2nd of the same year. The men met at Allegheny City and were led by R.A. Ammon or "Boss Ammon" as he was better known.[69]

---

[67] Willis F. Evans, *History of Berkeley County West Virginia*. (Bowie, Heritage Books, 1928),125.

[68] Philip S. Foner, *The Great Labor Uprising of 1877*. (New York, Pathfinder, 1977), 46.

[69] Terence V. Powderly, *Thirty Years of Labor*. (Columbus, Excelsior Publishing, 1889), 199.

In the evening of Monday, July 16th, "200 brakemen and firemen seized the depot and stopped all freight trains, allowing only passenger and mail trains to move."[70] All traffic came to a halt in Martinsburg. In return for John Garret's circular of a wage reduction, the Trainmen's Union issued their own. Edward Hungerford describes conditions of the men's lives as such, "The men were constantly being badly treated by merchants and boarding-house keepers along the line, the latter compelling them to pay inordinately high rates for meals and lodgings and the like. Even at home, they suffered from high rents, extravagant prices for groceries and other supplies and the demands of the money lenders."[71] Most of this, the workers understood and lived through. Those who did not work on the railroad were not aware of the situation. Both sides were now playing a war of words. The engines were uncoupled from the rest of the train and put into the roundhouse. The other train cars were run to the sidings or side tracks and out of the way of oncoming traffic. It was now clear that the men were serious and were not dismayed about what might happen to them. They demanded that no trains would move until the full pay cuts were restored to all the men.

Next, the local mayor of Martinsburg, Captain A.P. Shutt, was called to come and talk to the strikers. He asked for them to return to work or their homes and disperse. When the group just laughed at him, he then ordered the local police to arrest those who seemed to be in charge. Again, his orders were not obeyed as the police sided with the striking workers. The mayor and police withdrew, seeing that there was nothing they could do for the situation.

---

[70] Foner, *History of Labor Movement*, 465.

[71] Edward Hungerford, *The Story of the Baltimore and Ohio Railroad: 1827 to 1927.* (New York, Putnam, 1928), 134.

The scene at Martinsburg remained calm. The railroad yard was guarded by strikers overnight to prevent anyone from trying to take out any railroad cars. There had not been bloodshed or violence in the town. The operator at the telegraph office in Martinsburg sent a telegram to Baltimore to alert them of the situation. Captain Thomas B. Sharp, who was the General Master of Transportation for Baltimore and Ohio Railroad, was sent to Martinsburg to investigate. Sharp found the yard quiet, with guards sentried around on the lookout for any sign of movement.

In Wheeling, then the state capital of West Virginia, Baltimore and Ohio Railroad company officials were conferring with the governor of West Virginia. Jeremey Brecher said, "B&O officials in Wheeling went to see Governor Henry Mathews, took him to their company telegraph office, and waited while he wired Col. Charles Faulkner at Martinsburg." [72] The strength of the railroad was that it could make a governor send out the local militia. On the night of the 16th, he sent the following telegram to Faulkner, "have been requested to aid the authorities in Martinsburg to preserve the peace, if necessary do so with your company. Report to me the state of affairs."[73] The governor, and now the local militia captain, was aiding the railroad in securing the peace of the tracks. The railroad sits away from the road, so there was no interference to traffic other than train traffic. The governor had been told that there was another mob uprising in Berkeley County. He wired Faulkner the following telegram not long after the first, "In addition to the mob at Martinsburg, I understand another is gathering in the vicinity of Opequon."[74]

---

[72] Jeremy Brechner, *Strike!* (Oakland, PM Press, 2014), 12.

[73] Telegram from Governor Henry Mathews to Col. Charles J. Faulkner, July 16, 1877.

[74] Telegram from John King Jr. to Governor Henry Mathews, July 17, 1877.

Governor Mathews and John King were in talks during the uproar in Martinsburg. The governor, upon receiving confirmation of Faulkner at Martinsburg with his men, telegraphed King back with the following message,

"There are two military companies at Martinsburg, armed and supplied with ammunition. I have telegraphed my aide-de-camp, Colonel C.J. Faulkner, to aid the authorities with the companies to execute the law and suppress the riot. I will do all I can to preserve the peace and secure safety to your trains and railroad operations. Colonel Faulkner is directed to look also to Opequon."[75]

The next day, Colonel Faulkner wired Governor Mathews back with the following message once he had surveyed the scene, "Strikers have refused to allow trains to move either east or west from town. Do my orders extend any further than protecting the peace? If so, answer in full."[76] The strikers at this point were only stopping trains and disconnecting them from their cars. They were not in the town and were not looting or breaking any other laws other than stopping the railroad from running. Faulkner was informed that a mob was rioting but found the conditions at the railroad yard quite different. About an hour later, the governor wrote back to Faulkner with the following message, "Avoid using force if possible, but see that the law is executed and the riot suppressed. Give all necessary aid to the civil authorities. I rely on you to act discreetly and firmly. Look also to the Opequon."[77] There was no riot or mob at Opequon. It is uncertain why this was reported, but Faulkner found nothing to be spoken of at this junction and Martinsburg again was the source of the excitement.

---

[75] Telegram from Governor Henry Mathews to John King, Vice President of the B&O, July 17,1877.

[76] Telegram from Col. Charles J. Faulkner Jr., to Governor Henry Mathews, July 17, 1877.

The next order of business for Colonel Faulkner was to figure out how to get the trains moving again. The men in his company, numbered seventy-five, knew these men and were their neighbors, and possibly in some cases, family. It was hard for these men to open fire on people they knew and for a cause they actually supported. The way the railroad had treated the men the past couple of years was a source of frustration for even the people not working for the railroad. While trying to figure out what to do next, Faulkner wrote the following telegram to Mathews, "Must I protect men who are willing to run their trains, and see that the same are permitted to go east and west?"[78] In this telegram, Faulkner was hesitant to use any force. He did want to complete the mission for the governor but also knew his men would be reluctant to use weapons against them.

The governor's reply to Faulkner also tells more about where information was coming from. He replied, "I am informed that the rioters constitute a combination so strong that the civil authorities are powerless to enforce the law. If this is so, prevent any interference by the rioters with the men at work, and prevent obstruction of the train."[79] The civil authorities referred to were the mayor and his police force. Again, these were men that knew each other, so to arrest or shoot them was a tough decision as well, as they believed in their cause. He most likely was receiving information from Thomas Sharp, who was still in Martinsburg as the representative for the Baltimore and Ohio Railroad. Information that was coming from the telegraph office in Martinsburg was not entirely accurate of the situation. How else could he get the police force, militia, and maybe the army to break up the strike if he mischaracterized the situation?

---

[77] Telegram from Governor Henry Mathews to Col. Charles J. Faulkner Jr., July 17, 1877.

[78] Telegram from Col. Charles J. Faulkner to Governor Henry Mathews, July 17, 1877.

John King, Vice President of the Baltimore and Ohio Railroad, was in Baltimore at this time. King was receiving telegraphs from Thomas Sharp, who was in Martinsburg and observing the strike. This telegram from John King to Governor Mathews in Wheeling again shows the power of the railroad upon government. It read, "Would it not be well for you to issue a proclamation commanding the rioters to disperse and go to their houses at once and cease to interrupt the progress of trains upon the road. A proclamation issued by you and read or delivered by one of your officers would perhaps deter more violent movements."[80] Instead of the government deciding policy and direction, the railroad was making demands. Even though the railroad workers had a right to assemble peacefully, they were stopping business from operating. The railroad executives were wiring the governor what they wanted to happen instead of the governor telling them what the state was doing about the situation. It was an upside-down world regarding how business and government were operating.

The people of Martinsburg had not seen this much excitement since the end of the Civil War twelve years prior. There was much activity at the train depot and yard. The first group of strikers numbered about seventy-five. As the day went on, that number increased to about two hundred in all. "Meantime the assemblage of spectators and the array of strikers continued to increase. The balcony of the hotel which faced the line of railway, and the high land about and rising above the track, were literally crowded with greatly excited people, men, women, and children."[81] Like the Battle of Bull Run, these spectators did not anticipate that the excitement of the moment was about to turn ugly.

---

[79] Telegram from Govern Henry Mathews. to Col. Charles J. Faulkner Jr., July 17, 1877.

[80] Telegram from John King Jr. to Governor Henry Mathews, July 17, 1877.

Meanwhile, back near the railyard, Colonel Faulkner was deciding his next course of action. He had decided he was going to take one of the trains out of the station and resume business. With him was a fireman and engineer who could operate the train and who was not on strike. From the vicinity of the town and up the hill came fife and drum noise. Colonel Faulkner had put together his troops and was headed directly toward the roundhouse where the cars were being assembled. Up to a point, Faulkner had been successful. The train was moving slowly, flanked by his men with guns and bayonets. The crowd of strikers were hollering and swearing all the same but not stopping the train from moving. Mayor Shutt thought it best to have Colonel Faulkner address the crowd as to not interfere with the train movement. Faulkner stated to the men that he would see that their concerns were relayed to President Garrett and that they should not get in the way of any train being moved. The crowd then booed, hissed and laughed at him, not paying attention to his demands. Allan Pinkerton recounts the scene in Strikers, Communists, Tramps, and Detectives,

---

[81] Allan Pinkerton, *Strikers, Communists, Tramps and Detectives*. (New York, G.W. Carleton & Company, 1878.), 150.

"a militiaman named John Poisal, while sitting on the cow-catcher, particularly noticed the position of the switch-ball, which indicated that the train unless some change was made, would be thrown off the right track. Immediately jumping to the ground, musket in hand, he ran forward to the switch. William Vandergriff, one of the striking firemen, stood nigh, and had just swung the bar so as to send the engine in the wrong direction, and remained on watch to prevent its reversal. Join Poisal reached the spot in time and put out his hand towards the rod, when, amid the general confusion, Vandergriff's voice rang out loud and clear: "Don't touch that switch!". "I'm not going to see that train run on a siding if I can prevent it!"[82]

[82] Allan Pinkerton, *Strikers, Communists, Tramps and Detectives.* (New York, G.W. Carleton & Company, 1878.), 152-153.

At this point, Vandergriff had meant what he said and drew his small pocket pistol and fired two shots. Poisal's head was hit just above his ear, and the other bullet missed him completely. Men, women, and children that had been watching all the action fled the scene. The strikers and militiamen stayed. Poisal, in an act of revenge, raised his gun and discharged toward Vandergriff while another soldier fired at Vandergriff. Between the two men, Vandergriff was hit in the thigh and arm. Both men were removed from the scene and taken to their own houses.   Colonel Faulkner was powerless. "Tried to take the train out, was fired into. Had one man shot, and shot one man. The engineers and firemen left us, and we could not take the train out. No firemen or engineers will go."[83] He could not do anything to move the trains, and he tried. He knew that the men were not going to kill each other over the railroad issues. He decided that he and his men had enough. He told Thomas Sharp that he would be taking his men back to the armory to discharge them to their homes, and that is precisely what he did. The local militia was disbanded with one wounded and one striker on his deathbed.

Faulkner and Mathews corresponded about the events in the following telegrams:

---

[83] Telegram from Col. Charles J. Faulkner to Governor Henry Mathews, July 17, 1877.

Faulkner to Mathews, "It is impossible for me to do anything further with my company. Most of them are railroad men, and they will not respond. The force is too formidably for me to cope with."[84] Mathews back to Faulkner, "The peace must be preserved and law abiding citizens protected. Whatever force is necessary to accomplish this will be used. I can send if necessary a company in which there are no men who will be unwilling to aid in suppressing the riot and executing the law. Answer."[85] Faulkner to Mathews, "There is great excitement caused by the severe wounding of one of the strikers. Sympathy seems with them. Engineers and firemen are reluctant under this excitement to risk taking out trains. If you think such condition of things requires military force you will have to send if from other point than this, for reasons heretofore stated."[86] Colonel Faulkner felt defeated and probably disheartened that there had been bloodshed. That was never his intention or desire. He wanted to be able to restore order to Martinsburg without any violence.

At the same time, Thomas Sharp was communicating with Governor Mathews. He sent the following telegram,

"Capt. Faulkner is powerless to do anything, and has disbanded his troops, as they are principally railroad men. I beg you send troops here to quell the riot. I have 75 engines and trains here at a standstill. Rioters won't allow them to move. Two men have been shot, and all railway operations are at a standstill except passenger trains. Men at Keyser have struck and stopped trains."[87]

---

[84] Telegram from Col. Charles J. Faulkner to Governor Henry Mathews, July 17, 1877.

[85] Telegram from Govern Henry Mathews. to Col. Charles J. Faulkner Jr., July 17, 1877.

[86] Telegram from Col. Charles J. Faulkner to Governor Henry Mathews, July 17, 1877.

[87] Telegram from Thomas Sharp to Governor Henry Mathews, July 17, 1877.

Sharp again was dictating government policy by asking for troops to be sent to Martinsburg. There had been a reluctance to use federal force until all local resources had been used. After Faulkner failed to return Martinsburg back to the state it was in before the strike, he had no choice but to send other troops that did not know these men.

Governor Mathews sent the following telegram to Faulkner about his service, "I have heard with gratification of your speech to the rioters, and of your conduct in the discharge of the delicate and important duty with which you were entrusted. Your remarks were just what they should have been and your conduct characterized by wisdom and firmness, all that I would desire. Accept my thanks."[88] Faulkner was off the scene and returned home along with his troops.

---

[88] Telegram from Govern Henry Mathews. to Col. Charles J. Faulkner Jr., July 17, 1877.

On Wednesday, July 18, Governor Mathews sent from Wheeling, the Mathews Light Guard, commanded by Robert L. Delaplain with thirty-six men. Since these men were not from the area, it was believed that they would be able to do what the Berkeley Light Infantry was not, and that was to get the trains rolling again and the men back to work. Delaplain consulted with both Vice President, John King, town officials and railroad officials about the situation at Martinsburg. The men sent to break the strike were actually just like the strikers. They worked for industry and were farmers. They most likely understood their condition and sided with the strikers. Phillip S. Foner said this about their meeting, "The militia, composed of laborers and farmers, not only refused to shoot workers who were derailing freight trains, but fraternized with the railroad men, offering them their weapons."[89] These were men who could see themselves in each other and relate their grievances. They were all facing tough times together, even in two different cities. The depression not only affected Martinsburg but Wheeling as well. Delaplain, observing the reluctance of his militia to do anything about the strikers, wrote Governor Mathews via telegram. He stated that additional military assistance was needed in Martinsburg. The situation did not go as intended for Governor Mathews or Delaplain. Now, it seemed, was the time for a different course of action.

Governor Mathews had sent both local and state militia to quell the insurrection at Martinsburg. Neither one worked. His next move was unprecedented for its time. In the afternoon of July 18, he wired to President Rutherford B. Hayes. The wire stated,

---

[89] Foner, *History of Labor Movement*, 466.

"To His Excellency, R.B. Hayes, President of the United States, Washington, D.C. Owing to the unlawful combination of foreign and domestic violence now existing in Martinsburg and at other points along the line of the Baltimore and Ohio Railroad, it is impossible with any force at my command to execute the law of the State. I therefore call upon your Excellency for the assistance of the United States Military to protect the law abiding people of the State against domestic violence and to maintain the supremacy of the law. The Legislature is not now in session and could not be assembled in time to take action in the emergency. A force of from two to three hundred men should be sent without delay to Martinsburg, where my aid, Col. Delaplain will meet and confer with the officers in command."[90]

Governor Mathews had tried all he possibly could, and it did not work. He now was appealing to his last hope, the United States Government. The Secretary of War, George W. McCrary, wrote back to Governor Mathews with this, "Your dispatch to the President asking for troops is received. The President is averse to intervention unless it is clearly shown that the State is unable to suppress the insurrection. Please furnish a statement of facts. What force can the State raise? How strong are the insurgents?"[91] The president was reluctant just to send troops at the request of a governor. He wanted facts and more information from the source. He had been reading in the newspapers about the events in Martinsburg and the brewing of other issues around the country. At this time, he wanted to hear what was happening from a government official.

---

[90] Telegram from Govern Henry Mathews. to President Rutherford B. Hayes., July 18, 1877.

[91] Telegram from Secretary of War George McCray to Governor Henry Mathews,

President Hayes was not just receiving a telegram from Governor Mathews but also from the Baltimore and Ohio Railroad. John Garrett, President of the Baltimore and Ohio Railroad, was sending a telegram to urge the president to send troops per the request of the governor in the following message,

"I am informed that Governor Matthews, of West Virginia, has telegraphed your Excellency that, owing to unlawful combinations and domestic violence now existing at Martinsburg, and at other points along the line of the Baltimore and Ohio railroad, it is impossible for any force at his command to execute the laws of the State, and has therefore called upon the Government for assistance of the United States military in this great and serious emergency. I have the honor to urge that the application of Governor Matthews be immediately granted: it is impossible for the company to move any freight train, because of the open intimidation of strikers and attacks that they have made upon men in the service of the company who are willing to work, unless this difficulty is immediately stopped.

I apprehended the greatest consequences not only upon our line but upon all the lines in the country which, like ourselves, have been obliged to introduce measures of economy in these trying times for the preservation of the effectiveness of railway property.

May I ask your Excellency, if the application of Governor Matthews be granted, to have me immediately advised through the Secretary of War the points from which the troops will be sent, in order that no delay may occur in their transportation.

If I may be permitted to suggest, Fort McHenry and Washington are points nearest to the scenes of disturbance, and from which the movement can be made with greatest promptness and rapidity.

July 18, 1877.

It is proper to add that from full information on the subject I am aware the Governor of West Virginia has exerted all the means at his command to suppress the insurrection, and that this great national highway can only be restored for public use by the interposition of United States forces.

From an imperative sense of duty I am compelled to join in asking immediate action in order to prevent the rapid increase of the difficulties in use of lines between Washington City and Baltimore and Ohio River."[92]

The Baltimore and Ohio President was trying to persuade the President of the United States to send in federal troops. Not only that, but he also suggested where the men should come from and that they were from points nearest Martinsburg. The soldiers rode in on the train which only made sense since Garrett knew the line but went a bit far in dictating government policy.

The governor's reply he sent back to the Executive Mansion was this message,

> "The only organized force in the State consists of four companies. Two of them are at Martinsburg and in sympathy with the rioters, who are believed to be 800 strong. Another company is thirty-eight miles from a railroad, and only one company of forty-eight men is efficient. There is no organized militia in the State. I will send Colonel Delaplaine to see the President, if desired. He is at Martinsburg. I have been reluctant to call on the President, but deemed it necessary, to prevent bloodshed."[93]

---

[92] Telegram from John King, President of the Baltimore and Ohio Railroad to President Rutherford B. Hayes, July 18, 1877.

[93] Telegram from Govern Henry Mathews. to Secretary of War George McCrary., July 18, 1877.

Governor Mathews made it clear that he was at the mercy of the government. Mathews had tried and failed to put down the strike. Also, the state did not have an organized militia sufficient enough to aid. The only way this strike was going to end was if the president sent troops.

The president was now on board with sending troops to Martinsburg. He understood that Governor Mathews was unable to stop the strike with state resources. Also, the men were too close to the strikers, and a force outside of the state was needed.

While troops were being assembled to head to Martinsburg, the president was writing up a proclamation that those stopping the flow of train traffic return to their homes. All citizens of Martinsburg were to be in their homes by twelve o'clock on July 19th. This was to be circulated and read aloud to all those in the train yard. The time for demonstration seemed to be over. Here is the proclamation that was read aloud to the strikers:

"Whereas, It is provided in the Constitution of the United States that the United States shall protect every State in this Union, on application of the Legislature, or the Executive, when the Legislature cannot be convened, against domestic violence; and

Whereas, The Governor of the State of West Virginia has represented that domestic violence exists in said State, at Martinsburg, and at various other points along the line of the Baltimore and Ohio Railroad, in said State, which the authorities of said State are unable to suppress; and

Whereas, The laws of the United States require that in all cases of insurrection in any State, or of obstruction to the laws thereof, whenever it may be necessary, in the judgment of the President, he shall forthwith, by proclamation, command such insurgents to disperse and retire peaceably to their respective abodes within a limited time.

Now, therefore, I, Rutherford B. Hayes, President of the United States, do hereby admonish all good citizens of the United States, and all persons within the territory and jurisdiction thereof, against aiding, countenancing, abetting or taking part in such unlawful proceedings; and I do hereby warn all persons engaged in or connected with said domestic violence and obstruction of the law to disperse and retire peaceably to their respective abodes on or before 12 o'clock noon of the 19th day of July instant."[94]

At 6:30 AM on July 19th, Colonel Delaplaine and about three hundred United States troops arrived in Martinsburg. The newspapers at this point had been telling a story of looting, burning, pillaging and downright lies as to the conditions in Martinsburg. When they arrived, they were surprised to see that none of this was happening. There were just railroad cars lined up along the tracks but not in bad condition or molested. The men who were considered rioters were actually just striking for a living wage for themselves and their families. The depression had hit the country hard, and all they wanted was to be able to live off the work they were doing. The troops must have been in shock not to see the conditions that they were told were happening in Martinsburg.

---

[94] Proclamation from President Rutherford B. Hayes to the strikers in Martinsburg, July 19,1877.

The troops disembarked from the trains and went about the yard. Delaplaine had the president's proclamation printed so that it could be distributed to the men on strike. At noon, the federal troops took back the railroad and yards from the men. The strikers had already returned home before noon when the federal troops took back the yard. The trains were started back up and prepared to leave Martinsburg. The only issue with this was that the strikers were all home inside afraid of being arrested, and thus there was no one to run the trains.

The Sheriff of Berkeley County, Moses C. Nadenbousch, was put in charge of arresting the ringleaders. Officials from the Baltimore and Ohio Railroad gave the name of ten men who were considered ringleaders of the strike. Several of the strikers were arrested for their part. Martinsburg, for a brief moment, had been active in the start of something that had snowballed down the railroad line. The men may not have known it, but they demonstrated to the nation that employees could make demands upon their employers by going on strike. "In less than four days after the commencement of the strike on the Baltimore and Ohio Railroad, no inconsiderable portion of the territory of the United States was in the hands of the strikers; transportation was embargoed; shops closed, factories deserted, and the great marts which but a few days before had been so noisy, had become silent."[95] The men may not have realized, but their action affected men, women, and children from coast to coast. Their bravery to walk off the job and to stop capitalism was astonishing for the time. It was the classic story of David versus Goliath.

---

[95] Joseph A. Dacus, *Annals of the Great Strikes in the United States: A Reliable History and Graphic Description of the Causes and Thrilling Events of the Labor Strikes and Riots of 1877.* (Chicago, L.T. Palmer & Company, 1877), 23.

This section shows how powerful the railroad was to be able to dictate government policy. Not only did the railroad dictate policy, but it was their telegraph lines and transportation that moved the men around from the government, including troops. Their power was deep within the nation and felt by both the men working for them and those in political office. Martinsburg was a small, blue-collar town in 1877. It was a significant hub for the Baltimore and Ohio Railroad, and thus by the men going on strike, it meant the line was down from east to west. Martinsburg was important in this regard, and when the men went on strike, it affected the whole railroad system. If it had been an out-of-the-way lay station, the impact of Martinsburg would not have been so significant. Martinsburg was able to stop the flow of goods for four days in 1877, and the economic impact was felt not just in the small city, but along every major city, town, and hamlet.

Chapter 5-Baltimore & Pittsburgh Jump on Board

As Martinsburg was wrapping up its strike, other cities and locations across the United States were just starting their own demonstrations. Beginning in Louisville, Cumberland, Baltimore, Pittsburgh, Albany, Syracuse, Buffalo, Philadelphia, Reading, Scranton, Chicago, Bloomington, Aurora, Peoria, Decatur, Urbana, and St. Louis all took part in going on strike as well as many others in the West. In the end, cities in fourteen states went on strike.[96] Each area was different in how they went on strike, but each took part in what was known as the Great Strike of 1877.

Not all strikers were railroad men. Others taking part included the unemployed, coal miners, salt miners, canal workers, and factory workers among various other industries. The depression created labor and capital tensions unseen nationally, before 1877.

Baltimore, Maryland was situated on the Chesapeake Bay and was in a great geographical location to be the hub of the Baltimore and Ohio Railroad. From it flowed the road that led west to Cumberland, Maryland, followed by the national road onto Wheeling, West Virginia. The first tracks for the railroad were laid in Baltimore in 1827, and the westward progression began. The first stop on its line was Ellicott City, also in Maryland.

---

[96] Bill Barry. *The 1877 Railroad Strike in Baltimore.* (Baltimore, Create Space Independent, 2014), Kindle edition, chapter 1.

The workers in 1877 at the Baltimore railroad yards were either immigrants or of immigrant stock. After the Civil War, immigration was necessary for the Baltimore and Ohio Railroad to continue laying track and expanding its line. The Baltimore and Ohio even built a port in Baltimore to receive workers and dubbed it "Immigrant Pier."[97] The railroad, as well as other internal improvements, were built by laborers from Europe, but mainly the Irish in the case of the Baltimore and Ohio Railroad. As the railroad was constructed west, graves of the Irish who died from natural cause or disease could be found. Other immigrants who built the railroad sacrificed and sometimes paid with their lives. As the railroad was built westward and immigrants died of natural causes or disease, graveyards followed the tracks as well.

The trouble in Baltimore began before the Martinsburg strike. On the evening of July 15th, the engineers of several trains jumped off the cars and refused to move them any further. This was in reaction to the ten-percent pay cut that was to go into effect the following day. Those workers were arrested by the local police, and work continued on the line as usual with men who would run the trains. As the strike spread to Cumberland on July 20th, the governor called for state militia to travel to Cumberland by train. When the local citizens heard the call of the town siren for the militia, it must have set off a spark of rage. As the militia was getting ready in the armory, a crowd of citizens gathered outside. When the men tried to leave the armory, they were pelted with rocks and debris and heard the group yell "cries and cheers for the strikers."[98] The strike was now in full swing in the heart of the Baltimore and Ohio Railroad headquarters. The anger that flared across the country was on the door to the headquarters of the man who had cut the wages of all laborers within the company, President John W. Garrett. John Garrett was about to see the wrath of the working class up close and personal.

---

[97] Barry, 1877 Railroad Strike in Baltimore, kindle edition, chapter 1.

The men of the Sixth Maryland were ordered to leave the armory and head for the train station. When they did, they were met by a mob that not only swore and cussed at them but then began throwing stones. As man after man fell, the final straw was drawn, and a few shots were fired by the militia. Some of the protesters were shot upon, and a young man named Byrne was killed. The men of the Sixth Maryland kept up and moved forward toward Camden Station. They finally met up with the Fifth Maryland about a block from the station.

The men barricaded themselves inside the station. On the outside, the crowd grew larger and larger as word spread that some of the protesters had been shot in the streets. Protestors were busy burning down the dispatcher's office on Lee Street and setting fire to new passenger cars at the Camden Street Station. They even attempted multiple times to burn down the Camden Station without success.[99] The protesters were able to tear up train tracks along the lines to keep trains from moving. The anger that had been evident in Martinsburg was now tenfold in Baltimore. Trapped inside Camden Station was no other than Governor of Maryland, John Carroll, Baltimore Mayor, Ferdinand Latrobe and Vice President of the Baltimore and Ohio Railroad, John King. They had witnessed the full wrath of how labor was feeling about both unemployment and pay cuts.

[98] Philip S. Foner, *The Great Labor Uprising of 1877.* (New York: Pathfinder, 1977), 63.

[99] Edward Hungerford. *The Story of the Baltimore and Ohio Railroad: 1827-1927.* (New York: Putnam, 1927), 142-143.

The men who committed the uproar in Baltimore were not just railroad workers. The depression that was ongoing affected every industry in the nation. The anger was geared toward the railroad because of the way their greed was made public. James McCabe recalls in *The History of the Great Riots*, "The number of railroad employees engaged in the rioting here has from the first not exceeded 150; but at the outset of the affair they were joined by thousands of laborers and mechanics out of employment, and by the entire criminal classes of the city, eager for an occasion to plunder."[100] Baltimore produced men from various laborer positions as well as possible criminal elements. This made sure looting and plunder was a part of the equation, unlike in Martinsburg. In Martinsburg, the men wanted their pay cut reversed while Baltimore was looking at a different outcome altogether. When the opportunity arose, those of the criminal element most likely saw their opportunity to wreak havoc and to join in.

The last sound of the protesters was early the next morning on July 21st. A warehouse full of combustible material was set on fire, not in one place, but many. It awoke residents in the early morning at four AM. Afterward, federal troops, along with local, special police sworn in that day, moved into town and started to arrest those responsible and to enact martial law. Baltimore now quieted down from the excitement of two days. There were bodies to be buried and a town to rebuild just in two days of protest.

---

[100] James McCabe. *The History of the Great Riots*. (Philadelphia: National Publishing Co., 1877), 61.

Outside of Maryland and West Virginia, another city was about to go up in flames. On July 19th, the men working at Pittsburgh were told that they would be pulling double-headers. That is basically running double the number of cars than usual and being paid the same wage. This is in addition to the wage cut that was imposed a few days earlier. The first action of the day took place that morning when men refused to take the train cars out of the rail yard. When they disobeyed their supervisor, they were told they were fired. As the day went on, the remaining men went on strike and refused to move any cars or allow any cars to be moved, just like in Martinsburg.[101] The men who were on the trains being stopped decided to join their fellow trainmen and engineers and go on strike. By the end of the evening, the yard was full of trains and cars that were not being moved or serviced. The strike had continued northward to Pittsburgh and with the same passion as Martinsburg.

In the evening, the men gathered and came up with a list of demands before they would return to work. The demands included: wages being restored to before June 1, 1877 levels, reinstatement of anyone dismissed or arrested for their involvement in the strike, engineers and conductors receiving the same wage, running of double trains being abolished except coal trains, and every engine having a fireman.[102] These men had learned from the other strikes to come together as a union of men and trades and to make demands publicly. The workers had pulled together and struck for a reason, and not just for one reason. They came together like later unions and made their demands known.

---

[101] "War on the Tracks" *Pittsburgh Telegraph*, July 19,1877.

[102] Joseph Dacus. *Annals of the Great Strikes in the United States: A Reliable History and Graphic Description of the Causes and Thrilling Events of the Labor Strikes and Riots of 1877.* (Chicago: Beach, 1877),102-103.

The local government met with the leaders of the strike and the railroad to work out a deal. The railroad refused to accept even one demand of the strikers. More and more strikers and those who supported their cause gathered along the lines and near the stockyard. The tension was mounting since the local sheriff had already threatened to end the strike by whatever means necessary. It was estimated that ten thousand onlookers had gathered to watch what would happen between capital and labor in the great city of Pittsburgh.

On the 21st, the sheriff had issued warrants for the arrest of the supposed ringleaders of the strike. While executing his warrants, he was supported by the state militia. The sheriff was able to arrest about fifteen men in all when it all turned chaotic. The strikers rushed the sheriff and his men, and the militia opened fire on the strikers. Sixteen people were killed instantly. Some onlookers had been watching from the hills above for days. News of the firing on the men spread throughout the town very quickly, and it was said that not a house remained with a person inside. Mobs of people ransacked stores looking for weapons and armaments. The soldiers of Philadelphia that had fired upon the men were now locked up inside the roundhouse as more and more local people gathered in the rail yard looking for vengeance. A train car that was full of coke, used in making steel, was set ablaze, likely burning for days, and ran into the roundhouse which set the building on fire. The soldiers inside eventually escaped and were chased by a mob.[103] At this point, the town of Pittsburgh was in full anarchy. No police or militia fighting against the townspeople, and no other federal troops or state militia were in the area. More soldiers were being sent, but at the moment, the rioters, or more correctly a mob, had taken over the town. Not just buildings, but railroad property, buildings, and train cars had been set on fire. McCabe puts the damage at, "hundreds of cars, the extensive machine shops, two round houses, the depots and office of the Union Transfer Company, blacksmith shops, storehouses, and numerous other buildings making up the terminal facilities of this mammoth corporation. In the round houses were 125 first-class locomotives."[104] The events from first shot to a significant portion of the city in ruins were quick. Troops from Philadelphia had arrived quickly but did not stay away from violence. Once that first shot was fired, the people of

[103] McCabe. *The History of the Great Riots*, 76-101.

[104] Ibid., 101-102.

Pittsburgh reverted to the violence they knew, which was an eye for an eye. The depression had made opportunists of some, but anger geared toward others such as capital created the conditions that burned down cities.

The scene as portrayed in the press about the Martinsburg strike actually occurred in Pittsburgh. There were looting and fires galore with a majority of the city taking part at first. Men and women were seen up and down the street taking things from not only the freight cars and railroad shops but local merchants. Those in town not partaking in the looting were afraid the fires being set to cars and railroad property would extend to their property. It was unlike anything seen in the town before. One thousand miners from the nearby mine arrived on Sunday after receiving word that Philadelphia militia were killing the Pittsburgh strikers. They were easily calmed down and sent back after finding that Pittsburgh townspeople had taken care of the situation themselves. By Monday, July 23rd, local townspeople had come together and formed a posse to stop the riot. Their numbers were large enough to end any more looting or rioting. They had decided that the riot was too much even for them. At first, they were on the side of the strikers but not on the side of the looters. The end of the riot ended with the local town that was in favor at the start, to stop the whole affair by force. Pittsburgh received the most amount of damage out of Martinsburg and Baltimore. Some estimates at the time put the damage at fifty to sixty million dollars in 1877.

Baltimore and Pittsburgh showed how a strike can go from bad to worse in just seconds and with a different set of citizens, how reactions can change the course of history. When the three shots at Martinsburg took place on July 17th, the town could have erupted into chaos and disorder. The local militia was able to make sure that did not happen even after two men were severely wounded. Also, the men and women who were there reacted differently than in other locations. In Pittsburgh, this same event caused a mob to ruin the city and destroy a lot of property belonging to both the railroad and to the citizens. Baltimore reacted much the same way with the gunning down of citizens. All cities started off with a man on strike being shot, and all ended very differently. Martinsburg did not have any damage to buildings or property, and Pittsburgh lost half of its city and one of its major employers' building and locomotives in the Great Strike of 1877.

Martinsburg was never as big as Baltimore or Pittsburgh and never saw the wealth that those two bigger cities displayed. It was a small town filled with blue-collar workers just trying to make it through a day in 1877. Men like Andrew Carnegie brought not only jobs to Pittsburgh but immense wealth that was unparalleled. Martinsburg remained small with no huge benefactors, and much like the blue-collar town it was in 1877, it continued to stay that way.

Chapter 6-Outcome of Labor vs. Capital

The Great Railroad Strike of 1877 was indeed great for the number of people who joined in to confront the capital that was ruling their lives. Just about every major city in the United States was impacted by the strike, and many other small towns took part. It was an American event that affected the lives of just about every rich or poor citizen. Train service was halted along the East Coast at various points, mail service was delayed or stopped, passenger service was hung up by the strike, and goods did not make it to the market. Not only did the strike affect major railroads, but farmers, merchants, and industry of all sizes as the delivery of goods abruptly stopped. Other than the Civil War, most Americans during this era no doubt remembered the strike of 1877 and how it affected them personally.

The railroad held power in the United States much like Congress, or the president does today. It set its own rates and either made wealth or destroyed it. The power of the railroad was known to the people of the United States, and they did not like it. This was a power that was unchecked by the federal or state governments. It was allowed to run rampant and even aided the very politicians that should have been protecting the people and not the corporate interest. To illustrate this point, the railroads created and set the international time zones that are currently in use. They needed to have a consistent measure of time for trains not to collide, and a uniform set of pick up and drop offs, so the railways adopted time zones. This was the power of the railroads in action and the depth of their influence across the United States.

The men of 1877 were not backward, beaten down or uneducated. The workers along the tracks were firemen, brakemen, engineers, just like any other blue-collar workers. They were willing to work, but not for reduced pay and increased duties or double workloads. The men of the railways wanted to be treated fairly, and that was the way they would manage their jobs. When the workers lost not only ten percent of their pay but another ten percent less a year later, they knew they were not being treated honestly. The railroad was announcing a profit for the prior year, while at the same time telling the men they needed to reduce their pay to continue employing them. This was unacceptable, and the working men of the railroad would not stand for greed.

Martinsburg set the stage for the nation to go on strike. The demonstration that took place July 16th through the 19th was emulated in other parts of the country. A lot of different locations turned to violence and destruction, unlike Martinsburg. It was in Martinsburg that men stood up to capital and refused to move a train until their pay was restored. They did not ask for raises or bonuses or anything extra, but only to be able to live with the pay they were making the day before. This act was something entirely new to the United States, as there had not been a demonstration or act of resistance about work like the one that started in Martinsburg. The day before Martinsburg went on strike, the engineers near Baltimore walked off the job but did not go on what was considered a strike. It was entirely new to see men stop railroad cars from delivering their goods in protest for the way that capitalist was treating them. The men were no longer just a paycheck but an asset to the Baltimore and Ohio Railroad Company in Martinsburg. They were showing that the workers mattered and could not be treated any way the railroad pleased. If they were not going to get their pay restored, then they were going to make the railroad feel their pain by stopping the railroads' profits.

What made the situation worse for Martinsburg was the newspaper reports from sources other than local papers. Papers like the *New York Times* and *Harpers Weekly* talked about mobs, riots, insurrection, and the militia firing into the crowds. Although all of it had a sliver of truth, it was not the whole truth. When the outside world read the newspaper reports coming from Martinsburg, they were nowhere near accurate. Even though it is not covered in this book, the reports themselves could have incited violence to spread to Baltimore, Pittsburgh and beyond. The events at Martinsburg could have been the direct cause of loss of lives, train cars and buildings along the Baltimore and Ohio and other rail lines around the nation. Most assuredly, those in government such as Presidents Hayes and Governor Mathews were reading these reports as well as those at the Baltimore and Ohio Railroad.

Martinsburg was different in how the people went on strike. They did not want to set locomotives on fire or burn down buildings. They were simple people with only one condition, which was to work for a living wage. They had been overworked and underpaid but still saw their lives as working for the railroad. The men could have left their jobs and found a new employer. Even though the country, and Martinsburg, were in a depression, this is not what they did, and instead, put on a demonstration to stop their pay from being decreased. It was a chance they took, even if it meant being fired. There was no protection for their jobs from the government or their business. Also, there was no union protection in place to aid them if the railroad decided to let them go.

The cause of greed on the part of the railroad created an effect of a nationwide strike. The main railroad lines that decided to cut employees' paychecks instead of executive salaries or dividends was an error that the railroad created. The strikers at Martinsburg did not resort to violence to achieve their aim of a return of their salary. Their demonstration was meant to receive fair wages for fair work. Instead, they received four days of no work, one of their own was shot, and there was no return to benefits. The press, instead of focusing on Martinsburg, turned its attention to the other cities that had carnage and bloodshed. The railroad was able to move forward with giving up little, while the railroad workers seemed to have lost a lot more. By August, the strike was over, and the railroad had won. However, the battle between capital and labor was far from over.

Henry M. Mathews, Governor of West Virginia

Charles J. Faulkner, local attorney

Rutherford B. Hayes, President of the United States

John W. Garrett, President of the Baltimore and Ohio Railroad

Blockade of Engines at Martinsburg, WV 1877. Published in *Harpers Weekly*, August 11, 1877

Bibliography

Primary Sources
Camden, J.N. "Telegram to Governor Henry Matthews."
West Virginia Archives and History. Accessed January 28,
2017.
http://www.wvculture.org/history/labor/bandostrike04.html

Faulkner, Charles J. "Telegram to Governor Henry
Matthews." West Virginia Archives and History.
http://www.wvculture.org/history/labor/bandostrike05.html

Hayes, Rutherford B. "Diary of Rutherford B. Hayes."
Railroads and the Making of Modern America.
**http://railroads.unl.edu/documents/view_document.php?vie
ws[0]=Strike**.

King, Jr. John. "Letter to Governor Henry Matthews." West
Virginia Archives and History.
**http://www.wvculture.org/history/labor/bandostrike0
3.html**.

Martinsburg Statesmen "STRIKE" (Martinsburg, WV), July
21,1877.

Pittsburgh Telegraph. "War on the Tracks." July 19,1877.

Pittsburgh Telegraph. "The End Not Yet." July 21,1877.

Pittsburgh Telegraph. "The Riots Elsewhere." July 23,1877.

Shepherdstown Register "The STRIKE.", July 14, 1877.

Shepherdstown Register "The Great Uprising.", July 28, 1877.

Shepherdstown Register "The Labor Troubles.", August 4, 1877.
The Statesman "The Railroad Strike: The Full Particulars."
(Martinsburg, WV), July 24, 1877.

Secondary Sources

Aler, Veron F. *History of Martinsburg and Berkeley County, West Virginia*. Hagerstown, MD: Mail Publishing Company, 1888.

Baltimore American, July 16,1877. Accessed March 16, 2017.
    http://railroads.unl.edu/documents/view_document.
php?views%5B0%5D=Strike&rends
    %5B0%5D=newspaper&publication=Baltimore+Americ
an&id=rail.str.0003

Barry, Bill. *The 1877 Railroad Strike in Baltimore*. Baltimore: Create Space Independent Publishing, 2014. Kindle Edition.

Bellesiles, Michael A. *1877: America's Year of Living Violently*. New York: New Press, 2010. Kindle Edition.

Berkeley County Historical Society. "Berkeley County in the Civil War". *The Berkeley Journal, 26* (2000).

Berkeley County Historical Society. "Civil War Diaries and Letters from Berkeley County". *The Berkeley Journal, 29* (2003).

Berkeley County Historical Society. "Martinsburg, West Virginia During the Civil War". *The Berkeley Journal, 27* (2001).

Brecher, Jeremy. *Strike!* Oakland: PM Press, 2014.

Bruce, Robert V. *1877: Year of Violence*. Indianapolis: Bobbs-Merrill, 1959. Kindle Edition.

Cometti, Elizabeth, and Festus P. Summers. *The Thirty-Fifth State: A Documentary History of West Virginia*. Morgantown: West Virginia University Library, 1966.

Cooper, Jerry M. "THE ARMY AS STRIKEBREAKER." Labor History 18, no. 2 (Spring77 1977): 179.

Dacus, Jospeh A. *Annals of the Great Strikes in the United States: A Reliable History and Graphic Description of the Causes and Thrilling Events of the Labor Strikes and Riots of 1877*. Chicago: Beach, 1877.

------, J. A. *Revolution in Pennsylvania: A History of the Railroad Union Strike and the Great Uprising of 1877*. Red and Black Publishers, 2010.

Doherty, William T. *Berkeley County, U.S.A.: A Bicentennial History of a Virginia and West Virginia County, 1772-1972*. Parsons, W. Va.: McClain Print., 1972.

Dulles, Foster R. *The United States Since 1865*. Ann Arbor: University of Michigan, 1959.

Eggert, Gerald G. *Railroad Labor Disputes: The Beginnings of Federal Strike Policy*. Ann Arbor: University of Michigan Press, 1967.

Evans, Willis F. *History of Berkeley County, West Virginia*. Wheeling: Heritage Book, 1928.

Foner, Eric. *Reconstruction: America's Unfinished Revolution, 1863-1877*. New York: Harper Perennial, 2014. Kindle Edition.

Foner, Philip S. *History of the Labor Movement in the United States, Vol. 1*. New York: International, 1947.

------*The Great Labor Uprising of 1877*. New York: Pathfinder, 1977.

Gardiner, Mabel Henshaw., and Ann Henshaw Gardiner. *Chronicles of Old Berkeley, a Narrative History of a Virginia County from Its Beginnings to 1926*. Durham, NC: Seeman Press, 1938.

Hoffstadter, Richard. *American Violence: A Documentary History*. New York: Knopf, 1970. Kindle Edition.

Holbrook, Stewart. *The Story of American Railroads*. New York: Crown, 1947.

Hollis, Jeff. "The Baltimore and Ohio Railroad Story as Pertaining to Berkeley County". *The Berkeley Journal, 12*. (1983): 9-14.

Hungerford, Edward. *The Story of the Baltimore and Ohio Railroad: 1827-1927*. New York: Putnam, 1928.

Hunter, Robert. *Violence and the Labor Movement*. New York: Macmillan Co., 1914. Kindle Edition.

Leyburn, James G. *The Scotch-Irish: A Social History*. Chapel Hill: University of North Carolina Press, 1962.

Lingley, Charles Ramsdell. *The United States Since the Civil War*. New York: Harper, 1920. Kindle Edition.

McCabe, James D. *The History of the Great Riots*. Philadelphia: National Publishing Co., 1877.

Morris, Jr. Roy. *Fraud of the Century: Rutherford B. Hayes, Samuel Tilden, and the Stolen Election of 1876*. New York: Simon and Schuster, 2003. Kindle Edition.

Nevis, Allan. *The Emergence of Modern America: 1865-1878, Vol 8*. Chicago: Quadrangle, 1927.

"People's History: Great Strike of 1877." 2012.Turning the Tide 25 (3): 4.
   http://search.proquest.com/docview/1039541287?accou ntid=8289.

Philbrick Nathaniel. *The Last Stand: Custer, Sitting Bull, and the Battle of Little Bighorn.* New York: Viking, 2010.

Pinkerton, Allan. *Strikers, Communists, Tramps and Detectives.* New York: G.W. Carleton & Co., 1878. Kindle Edition.

Piper, Jessica. 2013. "The Great Railroad Strike of 1877: A Catalyst for the American Labor Movement". *The History Teacher* 47 (1). Society for History Education: 93–110.
   http://www.jstor.org/stable/43264188.

Powderly, Terence V. *Thirty Years of Labor: 1859-1889.* Columbus: Excelsior Publishing, 1889.

Rice, Otis K., Stephen Brown. *West Virginia: A History, 2nd ed.* Lexington: University Press of Kentucky, 1994.

Rice, Otis. K. *West Virginia: The State and Its People.* Parsons: McClain Printing, 1972.

Silvius, Don. "Between the Lines: The War Comes to Berkeley County, April-May 1861"(2016).

Slap, Andrew. *Reconstructing Appalachia: The Civil War's Aftermath.* Lexington: University Press of Kentucky, 2010.

Smith, Page. *The Rise of Industrial America: A Peoples History of the Post-Reconstruction Era, Vol. 6.* New York: Penguin Books, 1984.

Stampp, Kenneth. M. *The Era of Reconstruction: 1865-1877.* New York: Vintage, 1965.

Trefousse, Hans L. *Rutherford B. Hayes.* New York: Heny Holt & Co., 2002.

Vance. J.D. *Hillhilly Elegy: A Memoir of a Family and Culture in Crisis.* New York: Harper Collins, 2016.

Ware, Norman J. *The Labor Movement in the United States:1860-1895.* New York: Vintage Books, 1929.

West Virginia Population by Race," West Virginia Population by Race, 2015, accessed April 09, 2017,
http://www.wvculture.org/history/teacherresources/censuspopulationrace.html.

Made in the USA
Middletown, DE
17 August 2021